STOKE-ON-TRENT
A HISTORY

The view towards Etruria Vale from Hartshill Bank in about 1950 shows the impact of the steelworks.

STOKE-ON-TRENT
A HISTORY

Alan Taylor

Phillimore

2003

Published by
PHILLIMORE & CO. LTD
Shopwyke Manor Barn, Chichester, West Sussex

ISBN 1 86077 245 5

Printed and bound in Great Britain by
THE CROMWELL PRESS
Trowbridge, Wiltshire

For
Jan, Josh and Sam

Contents

List of Illustrations

Frontispiece: The view towards Etruria Vale from Hartshill Bank, *c.*1950

Acknowledgements

Illustrations are an important part of any volume such as this and I would like to thank the following for their generosity and contributions.

Brenda and Syd Bailey, 82; David Barker, 9, 11, 16, 20, 24, 26-7, 29, 33; the estate of Fred Leigh, 69, 70-3, 75, 87; Donald Morris, 4, 68, 104-8; the Nursing History Group, 42-3, 46, 49, 90-1; Paul O'Donnell, 109-12; The *Sentinel*, 28, 77, 79; Eveline Shaw, 76; Denis Thorpe and *The Guardian*, 101. Illustrations 3, 8, 17, 19 and 23 are from Plot's *Natural History of Staffordshire*. Images 2, 5, 7, 10, 13-15, 18, 21-2, 44-5, 84, 98-9, 102, 113-15 were taken by myself. Illustrations 64, 66 and 73 are accredited to William Blake, one of the most proficient photographers of north Staffordshire during the first half of the 20th century. He was a photographer with a social conscience and his works illustrate the living and working conditions of the people of the Potteries more clearly than any other photographer of the period. A large body of his work is now in The Potteries Museum & Art Gallery alongside a large archive of the work of Donald Morris, who documented the changing face of the Potteries during the closing decades of the century.

Introduction

The history of Stoke-on-Trent should not be seen in isolation from its surroundings. This book concentrates on the region that has become known as the Potteries as well as the land and communities that surround it. The area has developed from one containing numerous settlements, each of which was separate from the rest, to a large conurbation complete with dormitory towns. At some point the smaller communities have been swallowed up in the growth of the modern city; others have fought long and hard to retain their own identity. The borough of Newcastle-under-Lyme is chief amongst these although its infrastructure is as dependent on its neighbour as Stoke is on it.

An account such as this by its nature leaves out such a lot of the history of the area. I apologise in advance for these omissions. I have, I hope, achieved a balance between the histories

1 The source of the River Trent near Biddulph.

2 The plain headstone marks the burial place of Josiah Wedgwood in Stoke churchyard.

of institutions, the histories of locations and buildings and the histories of the people. Like the outlying communities, these too must be given account. They too contribute to the identity of the city today.

Ironically with the Potteries, those elements I have used to give some form of unity to the story also serve to highlight the differences within Stoke-on-Trent. The city has developed along a, broadly speaking, north to south axis with the six towns of Tunstall, Burslem, Hanley, Stoke, Fenton and Longton. Each of these towns held a strong sense of civic identity during the 19th century; one or more was resisting federation until 1910. The impressive array of town halls, parks and other civic amenities has each served to proclaim the existence of the town to the outside world. Since federation, the inhabitants have maintained a loyalty to their hometown. Fenton has perhaps suffered more than its neighbours due to Bennett's neglect of the town in his stories of the Potteries. A journey around

Fenton today illustrates the real neglect the town has suffered, especially when compared with the regeneration of and investment in Hanley and Stoke.

This area of the north Midlands is rich in history. Archaeological finds from the Palaeolithic era clearly indicate that humankind was active in the region. Although a nomadic people, their seasonal occupations of caves in the Manifold Valley have left us a distinct picture of their lifestyle and in particular their burial customs. From the Bridestones we have evidence of a more enlightened view on life and death. With the Romans we see the first beginnings of industry and in particular the early development of pottery kilns. Little did these potters, possibly itinerant and part of the Roman legions, know how their technology was to develop into an industry that became worldwide in its achievements. What is surprising is that it took so long. There is so little surviving evidence of a pottery industry until the 16th and 17th centuries. Even then

3 The throwing room at Etruria, a male preserve in the pottery workplace.

it was not an organised industry requiring specialist buildings with strictly organised labour. It developed as a cottage industry to supplement meagre incomes and at best to serve local demand. Only with the cutting of the Trent and Mersey Canal by Josiah Wedgwood did the potential of the industry come to be realised. Wedgwood built his workforce a model village so that they could work in the purpose-built factory on his estates – the industrial age had arrived.

Other accounts of the pottery industry do it far better justice than I have been able to in these pages. But it was not the only industry

to develop in the city. Coal mining and steel formed the other two core industries. It was no accident that the pottery industry sprang up on rich coalfields, and when the local clay became more scarce and, crucially, of too poor a quality to sustain the technological developments, the decision was made to remain in north Staffordshire because of the abundance of good quality coal. The canal could be used to import the higher quality clays from the south west, as it could be used to ship out the products of the industry to the ports of Liverpool and hence America, and to Hull and from there to Europe.

4 Arthur Egerton carries out the delicate task of stacking the saggars in the kiln at Burgess and Leigh in Middleport in 1964.

The coal and steel industries in particular developed with the active participation of the local gentry and aristocracy. From the selling of mineral rights through to massive investment in the modernisation of technology, the likes of the Duke of Sutherland have been at the forefront of the development of these industries. Some would argue that the patriarchal and dynastic involvement of these families served to the longer-term detriment of the industries. But the local pottery industry was organised on just such lines and continued to grow until the mid-20th century. Indeed, the organisation and development of labour relations within the pottery industry was at variance with much of industry as a whole.

5 The rebuilt arches of the old church in Stoke churchyard (above) and a stone (right) marking the site of the altar.

The following also includes some account of the period from the Norman Conquest to the 15th century. Again, individuals, whose sphere of activities took them on to national and international levels, impacted on the area. Through their fortunes and misfortunes local religious houses prospered or suffered and so too did the local economy and community. Recent archaeological work, particularly at Hulton Abbey and Berryhill, which again cannot be given proper justice in this account, has thrown much light on this period of history. We can now approach the complex social structures with better understanding, so that the

6 Times Square was first set out in 1789 and Longton's first town hall was built there in 1844. The current building dates from 1863 and features a *porte-cochère*. The building narrowly avoided demolition and was saved by the action of local people.

ephemeral histories of the Knight's Templar and the Men of Biddle (Biddulph) can be considered as a part of the broader picture.

The contemporary history of the area, the post-war history, is deserving of a volume in its own right. The Potteries as a region has developed into a complex society still in search of a post-industrial identity. Arguably, for far too long the area depended upon its traditional core industries. Of these coal and steel have now totally disappeared. The last steel from Shelton Bar was rolled in April 2000 and years after the long struggle of the miners in 1984-5, the fears of their union leaders have been

realised. Pits across the country have been closed down and there are no operative pits in north Staffordshire. Even the pottery industry now faces an uncertain future as the smaller companies have disappeared and the larger corporations shift production overseas. Stoke has been left with little. It has been by-passed by so many regeneration projects that have established new industrial bases in the likes of Derby. Now it struggles to attract new investment that will bring meaningful numbers of jobs to the area. A cultural strategy has been designed to promote the city as a place of culture and heritage worth visiting in

7   Stoke Town Hall, built between 1834 and 1850. The King's Hall was built to the rear in 1911. Outside the entrance to the King's Hall stands a brick cenotaph that replaced an older stone cenotaph resembling the one in Whitehall in the 1930s.

preference to Manchester, Birmingham and Sheffield. In these areas it has much to offer. From theatres accepting West End productions to community art groups working in schools and youth centres, there is a vibrant creative scene in modern Stoke. Nightclubs have helped to keep the city on the map but although they attract clubbers from around the country, they suffer from the lack of image the city suffers in general. A recent flourish in bar-clubs goes without comment in the city, but the trend towards these and away from the larger clubs is one now being noted elsewhere in the country. There was once a club in Hose Street in Tunstall called 'The Golden Torch'. It created an identity that young people were proud of and drew a massive following from around Britain. The city needs to hold up its torch in this field as in others, a salutary lesson for the future.

One

Early History

There have been two significant finds suggesting human activity during the Palaeolithic period in what was to become the Midlands area. Two hand axes, one from Shenstone and one from Drayton Bassett, have been confirmed from the Lower Palaeolithic period, suggesting human activities at the time of the last glaciation of the area that reached its peak around 26,000 to 15,000 BC. There is also evidence from the Manifold Valley. Flint tools and animal bones suggest occupation on several occasions from about 11,000 years ago and human remains dating back about 12,000 years have been excavated at Elderbush Cave. Other caves in the valley have been occupied at various times and some have been used as burial sites. A single adult of the late Neolithic to early Bronze Ages was buried in Thor's Cave, one of the most spectacular caves in the area; four adults and one child were discovered in Old Hannah's Cave, although these have not been positively dated. One of the largest such finds however, was in the Cheshire Wood Cave, where two adults aged between 25 and 30 and two children aged between 2 and 5 years, all dating from about 5,000 years ago, were found amongst numerous sherds of pot.

The evidence for human occupation remains small however. This is hardly surprising if Clark's estimate of the total population of England and Wales in the Mesolithic era as between 3 to 4,000 is accurate.[1] The population during this period was nomadic. The cave occupations may have been seasonal as the hunters followed their prey. This was not a farming society. Later finds include tools fashioned for working leather, probably for clothing, such as at Wetton Mill Minor where the remains of an adult male and adult female, an adolescent girl and 11 children of the early Bronze Age were found.

The Neolithic settlers have left a little more in the way of evidence. This suggests a more settled lifestyle. Mankind no longer followed the herds but began to domesticate animals, raising them near to the simple structures they erected. The settlers began to articulate themselves in new ways, particularly in their spirituality and their care for the dead. The end of the Neolithic period and the beginning of the Bronze Age see the arrival in the landscape of the barrow or burial mound. King's Low at Tixall was excavated during the late 1980s and early 1990s. A cinerary urn dating from about 3,600 years ago buried under a low mound was covered with a larger mound of sand and turf when a second cinerary urn was buried on the site. Two wooden stakes accompanied the earlier burial, their significance being unknown, perhaps ritualistic. The mound was raised a third time but no evidence of a burial has survived in the highly acidic soil.

Over one hundred round barrows survive, predominantly in the Staffordshire Moorlands region. This does not suggest automatically that these settlers favoured the upland areas. The broad

8   The Bridestones on the Staffordshire and Cheshire border, all that remains of a once significant long barrow.

plain of the Midlands has been extensively farmed and industrialised, processes that have destroyed much of the archaeological evidence. Revisionist ideas now suggest that the Midlands was a trade route before the Romans arrived with their road systems. If this were the case then there would have been more evidence, if only in the form of mounds, of occupation in the region. Even Plot, writing in the late 17th century, records the presence of mounds along Watling Street. These may have been burial sites.

One further site worthy of mention in the vicinity is that known as the Bridestones on the Cheshire border. Thought to date from about 3,000 BC, these upright stones are the remains of a long barrow. Aligned east to west, there is a chamber in the eastern end with two portal stones over ten feet high. It is thought two other chambers along with the mound were destroyed during excavations carried out in the 18th century. The name is thought to be derived from the goddess Bride or Brighid.

9   Thor's Cave in the Manifold Valley.

Probably the first inhabited settlement within the boundaries of modern Stoke-on-Trent was that at Penkhull, which was first occupied about two and a half thousand years ago. A cinerary urn dating from about 1,800 BC, dug up during the construction of the garden village, adds to the arrowhead of about 2,500 to 2,000 BC found in Chamberlain Avenue, suggesting that the settlement centred around the St Thomas' Place area. It was not an isolated community however, despite its elevated position above the surrounding ground. Burial mounds were reported in 'Bury Hill' and Fenton Low by Robert Garner in 1844.[2] The Berryhill area has also yielded flint tools as well as Bronze-Age axeheads.

The Romans arrived in the region in about AD46. They established military bases at

Rocester, Chesterton, Wall and Penkridge. Chesterton enjoyed only a short occupation during the Flavian period of the late first to early second centuries. It was, however, a strategic site, guarding the road from Uttoxeter through to Cheshire, important because of the salt the Romans mined from the neighbouring region. Rocester underwent three phases of building and expansion between about AD140 and 200 and archaeological excavations have revealed a massive timber barracks building. Pottery and glass have also been recovered from the site. We also know that the inhabitants enjoyed a diet that included wheat, barley, beef, lamb, ham and chicken.

Rather than introduce agriculture to the area, the Romans developed and expanded on principles already practised by the local inhabitants. In some areas villas were built to house wealthier or important citizens and in some cases to act as a hub to an estate. Two villas have been excavated in the north Staffordshire region. That at Hales, near to the Shropshire border town of Market Drayton, was built of stone during the first century. It is rectangular in form with a corridor connecting the four rooms. A bath house was added in the second century. The second villa was at Engleton near to Penkridge, the Roman town of Pennocrucium. Built in the second century on a winged corridor house plan, it too had a bath house, obviously an important feature in Roman domestic arrangements even in this part of the empire. A boundary ditch also surrounded the villa. Undoubtedly inhabitants of the area attempted to maintain a lifestyle similar to that they enjoyed during the Romano-British period but such a lifestyle was, like the empire, receding. Villas such as these were ultimately abandoned, as they became more expensive to maintain during the late fourth and early fifth centuries, the building materials being later re-used on Saxon structures.

In 1960, in the garden of a house in Lightwood Road, Longton, a hoard of coins was discovered. Totalling 2,461, the hoard comprised 1,739 regular issue coins and 722 irregular coins or 'barbarous radiates'. One of the most common coins of the third century was the radiate carrying an image of the current emperor wearing a crown of rays, hence the name of the coin. Throughout the century the silver content of the radiates was reduced and in 274 the coinage was reformed by Aurelius. Since the introduction of an official coinage, forgeries had been common. In northern Europe forgers exploited the short supply of the new coinage, supplying the market with the 'barbarous radiates'. They can be distinguished from the official coins by their poor workmanship and finishing. The Lightwood hoard was buried sometime during the reign of the Emperor Probus (276–82) and included two silver bracelets in the earthenware pot in which the whole was buried. The reasons why the coins and bracelets were buried are not known. In times of trouble and uncertainty, burial of valuable possessions was a common practice, the owner usually returning to retrieve their hoard later.

Another significant find of the Roman period is the pottery kiln at Trent Vale. This is one of the earliest examples of ceramic production in the area. It dates from the first century AD and was excavated in the 1950s. Cooking pots were still in the kiln and there were a number of vessels of local clay faced with gravel. Other finds from the site include lamp holders, platters, bowls, flagons and mortaria. There was also a quantity of Samian ware from southern Gaul that would have been the possession of the people who worked the kiln.

A significant feature introduced into the landscape by the Romans was the road. Watling Street, perhaps the most famous

10 The remains of a Saxon cross shaft re-erected in Stoke churchyard in 1935 to mark the Silver Jubilee of George V in 1935.

Roman road, runs through Staffordshire connecting London and North Wales. At Letocetum, near Lichfield and the site of one of the most complete Roman town bath houses in Britain, Ryknild Street, the major route between Yorkshire and Gloucestershire, crosses Watling Street. A further road ran from Derby through Rocester and Chesterton, possibly to the salt mines of Cheshire. A road from the Moorlands through Holditch at Chesterton, and possibly through Leominchistrete near Market Drayton, would have been a major north-south throughway. These Roman roads have influenced major communication routes in later centuries.

With the collapse of the empire during the fifth century, the Roman troops withdrew from Britain, leaving behind a legacy that was to have long lasting effects. Many of the leaders of the indigenous population had embraced Roman lifestyles, beliefs and systems. The Celts, who had been driven from their land, never recovered to reclaim their birthrights in Britain and new settlers, the Anglo-Saxons, moved in. The Celts were not totally displaced and their influence can be found in place-names. Despite the colonisation of the uplands by the Angles, the majority of the settlers in these regions remained British. Hints, derived from the Celtic 'hynt' meaning road, can be found near to Watling Street; the neighbouring community of Weeford, derived from the Anglian description of a pagan temple is further evidence of a co-existence between the indigenous peoples and the new settlers. Similarly, Eccleshall, the root of which is Celtic for church, suggests another example. In north-west Staffordshire there are several examples of the name Walton, which is commonly accepted as 'village of the Britons'. Penkhull, the settlement served by the nearby church at Stoke, was possibly a British hill-top settlement, 'pencet' derived from

the British for 'end of the wood', and the Old English 'hyll'.[3] The Anglians were not nomadic peoples and in Staffordshire they occupied the Trent Valley and surrounding areas. Small farming communities were established such as that at Catholme where 66 wooden buildings were grouped into holdings, each enclosed by a ditch and connected by trackways. A number of these buildings had raised floors, suggesting use as a grain store, whilst others had sunken floors and were used as workshops. Spinning whorls and loom weights indicate their use for spinning and weaving. Society at the time was ordered along the lines of a peasantry and aristocratic warrior class with a growing grouping of skilled craftsmen supplying the wealthy with jewellery. Crafts such as pottery remained a domestic skill.

The times were uncertain and settlements such as this needed the security of earthworks as the Roman garrisons declined and disappeared. Staffordshire was a part of the kingdom of Mercia, whose chief royal residence was at Tamworth and earliest Christian cathedral was at Lichfield. By the mid-800s, Viking incursions increased and their stays were more prolonged. Historians are uncertain exactly how much of the area that was later to become Staffordshire was controlled by the Danes. Watling Street was the boundary between unoccupied England and the Danelaw but there are few settlements with Danish roots suggesting widespread occupation so far west in Staffordshire. Ethelfleda, sister of Edward of Wessex, established fortresses at Tamworth and Stafford, having won the lands back from the Danes. After her death in 918, the Mercians submitted to her brother bringing the Mercian kingdom to an end. It is possible that the Wessex shire system of governance was introduced at this time. In 926 Editha, sister of King Athelstan, married the Danish King Sihtric at Tamworth.

Evidence of the region's pagan roots is to be found mostly in the Trent valley. Settlements outside of the valley, for which more substantial evidence survives, indicate a Christianised society. At Wednesbury, in the south of the county, the parish church stands in what are possibly the remains of an Iron-Age hillfort. The church is thought to have replaced an earlier pagan temple. Evidence from around Letocetum suggests that area given by the Mercian kings already had a significant church before St Chad established his cathedral there in about 670. Throughout the county there are examples of pre-Conquest crosses. The most striking are Wolverhampton, Leek and Ilam. Of these, that at Wolverhampton is about 14 feet high with an elaborate decoration carved into it and dates from about 850. The church is dated to about 994, suggesting that the cross was a preaching cross. At Stoke, fragments of a Saxon cross were discovered in 1876 in the churchyard and were re-erected by Percy Adams of Woore Manor to commemorate the Silver Jubilee of George V in 1935.[4] Carved in Millstone Grit from the Wetley Moor area, the decoration on the cross is reminiscent of that at Leek and Ilam.[5] The term Stoke is Old English for 'a place' and in particular a holy place, strongly suggesting that this area was perhaps one in which indigenous peoples may have co-existed with new settlers who eventually erected the cross on a religious site prior to the building of a church. The church stood in the floodplain of the Trent near to the road from Derby and is mentioned in Domesday Book. When the old church was

11 Cross shaft at Leek, one of a pair, that stands over ten feet high and has a characteristic waistband.

demolished in 1829 a corbel head was found inscribed indistinctly with the numerals DCCCI taken by some as evidence that an older stone structure had been on the site.[6] This church served the neighbouring settlement at Penkhull, which is also referred to in Domesday. A settlement at Stoke is not mentioned.

Two

The Medieval Period

The Norman Conquest of Britain did not affect Staffordshire until about 1070. Rebellions were mercilessly suppressed and the region was subjected to William's scorched earth policy. About 62 vills were described as waste in Domesday, almost twenty per cent of the county's total. Of these 62, about two thirds were north of Stafford. As a result of the rebellions, motte and bailey castles were built at Chester, Stafford, Dudley and Tutbury.

Domesday Book affords a precise insight to the nature of the county. It was sparsely populated compared to other counties, with extensive woodlands and largely uninhabited uplands. What agriculture there was seems to have been subsistence and there was little industry. Palliser calculates that there were 980 plough teams recorded, as little as half the number recorded in neighbouring Shropshire. This means that if the conventional figure of 120 acres per plough team is reliable then only 120,000 acres in the county were used for arable farming.[1] There are reasons to suspect that Domesday is not an accurate picture of Staffordshire as the survey took little notice of livestock farming, for which the county is better known. Despite this, however, there was a large number of windmills recorded in the county suggesting that arable farming was important to the local economy. Later ecclesiastical surveys indicate a large class of rent paying tenants in the county, overlooked or omitted by the Domesday surveyors.

The Normans introduced a new system of governing the land. By the time of Domesday, William was the chief landowner in the county. Owning the remainder of the land were the Earl of Shrewsbury, Henry de Ferrers, Robert de Stafford, William fitz Ansculf and the Bishop of Chester and Lichfield. These lords imposed the manorial system under which the lords owed allegiance directly to the king or to an intermediary aristocrat.

Of the towns that form the modern city of Stoke there is patchy evidence in Domesday. Tunstall was not mentioned. It seems likely that it was accounted for either within Thursfield (Wolstanton) or Chell. They were part of the lordship held by Richard the Forester. By 1200 Aline and Engenulph de Gresley held both Tunstall and Chell. Both these settlements included large tracts of woodland, part of the Forest of Lyme, reflecting the creation of royal forests by William I in Staffordshire. These forests, by no means continuous woodland, remained important sources of income for the Crown until the Elizabethan period. The land in this area is heavy clay, not suitable for arable farming but able to sustain pasture.

Burslem is listed in Domesday Book and was assessed for a third of a hide belonging to Robert de Stafford. Woodland again is listed but the details for Burslem are scarce, perhaps because it was mostly waste.

Hanley is nowhere recorded until 1212, when William of Hanley is listed as a royal sokeman (having local rights of jurisdiction) in the feudal township.[8] He still held the vill in 1236 upon paying a rent of 6s. to the king through Newcastle. This included a level of security provided by the castle.

There has been confusion over Fenton as at the time the area was divided into Fenton Vivian or Little Fenton and Fenton Culvert or Great Fenton. It is almost certainly the former listed in Domesday as thane land amounting to about thirty acres held by the Saxon Alward. The area was described by the Domesday surveyors as waste.

Longton is not noticed in official documents until the early 13th century, when Ranulph de Bevill granted Longton stream to the priory at Trentham.[3] The priory farmed much of the land in the Longton area by the mid-1200s and raised large flocks of sheep. Before 1236, when the manor was annexed to Newcastle, Ranulph de Bevill held it at a rent of 5s.

These settlements were connected by meandering tracks, many of them undoubtedly ancient by 1086. Originally they may have been paths for moving livestock. Their leisurely and wandering line is often reflected in the modern street system. The Roman Derby to Chesterton road, also known in medieval times as Rycknield Street, was also still in use as a major thoroughfare during this period.

There are no significant buildings or remains surviving from the post-Conquest years within the Stoke-on-Trent boundary. The Normans introduced a system of castles, notably at Tutbury, Tamworth, Stafford and Dudley. At Eccleshall the bishops of Lichfield and Coventry were given royal permission to fortify their episcopal palace in 1200. Bishop Walter de Langton rebuilt it between 1310 and 1315. The castle from which Newcastle derives its name was not built until the 12th century and of it there are very few remains.[4] Under the

rule of the Normans the balance of power was very much in favour of Newcastle and this balance in one form or another, should not be underestimated throughout the history of the north Staffordshire area. Clearly, many of the manors in the area owed some allegiance to Newcastle by the mid-1230s. Apart from a handful of moated sites and platforms, there are few other secular remains from which to draw evidence for this period.

During the 12th and 13th centuries the population grew and more land was settled. Manorial records frequently mention 'assarts', plots of land cleared of trees for cultivation and settlement. Tenants were also being expected to remove from their land the threat of flooding. Records relating to grants of land in the Manifold Valley include clauses about drains and sluices. As water became a more manageable resource, the number of mills increased. There were already 63 watermills in the county by 1086. From 1300 these were supplemented by windmills, indicating a growing demand for grain.

But it was the great religious houses that provided the impetus for land clearance. Typically, the Cistercians settled in the moorland regions, establishing houses at Croxden in 1179, Dieulacres in 1214 and at Hulton in 1219. An Augustinian priory was founded at Trentham in 1150. Both Hulton and Trentham depended on wool for a large part of their income and a number of pasture disputes broke out in the middle of the 13th century.

The Cistercians were voracious in their agrarian intent. Their estates were large and managed through dependent farms and granges and the order was not adverse to clearing existing villages and hamlets to make way for these farms. Rushton itself was cleared to make way for a grange for Hulton Abbey. Although there is no archaeological evidence, it is thought

12   Rushton Grange in about 1800. The Grange had been a part of the estates of Hulton Abbey.

that the ecclesiastical enclave itself removed at least a part of the very small settlement at Hulton.[5] Rushton and Hulton are at opposite ends of a strip of land and, despite the place-names suggesting a fairly open landscape, there was a large amount of woodland on the lands granted to the newly founded abbey. There was little agriculture and the communities were scarcely populated.

Hulton Abbey was established under the patronage of Henry of Audley. It was one of the last Cistercian houses in Britain. The monks who were to form the community had been selected and were ordained in 1218 or 1219 and building work must have commenced soon after. The abbot of the neighbouring house at Croxden complained in 1220 to the Chapter-General of the close proximity of Hulton, having already expressed concern over Dieulacres at Leek. The foundation charter that assigned lands and rights to Hulton was signed in 1223.

Hulton's was not a generous endowment. Initially estates at Abbey Hulton, Sneyd Green,

Cobridge, Meir Heath and Normacot were supplemented with smaller endowments in Bucknall made by other patrons. In 1232 the manor of Mixon and Bradnop, a remote and desolate but nevertheless valuable and produc-tive place east of Leek, was added. These lands remained the major source of income for the establishment up until its dissolution in 1538. Audley also made an allowance of £6 14s. per annum. This represented about a third of the abbey's income. After 1232 the monks were required to say mass daily and in perpetuity for the Audley family and their descendants. During the Baronial Wars of the mid-13th century balances of power shifted and the Audleys lost some of their power and subsequently establishments like Hulton Abbey lost some of their protection. Matters came to a head in 1268 when the abbot of Hulton claimed to have been kidnapped whilst on his way to Stafford and held until the ransom of 40s. had been paid. The case was dropped when the abbot refused to travel again to Stafford to give evidence.

13 The cross shaft in Trentham churchyard that has traditionally marked the resting place of the body of St Werburgh when it was moved to Chester.

Following a series of disastrous crop failures, the Black Death reached north Staffordshire in 1349. The religious communities felt its effects as much as the secular. The Audleys attempted to increase the abbey's income with the endowment of more estates, but the abbey was unable to realise the potential of these. It fell into considerable debt and was ordered by the king to forfeit livestock and land in order to pay off the debt. This state of affairs was short-lived however as the continued patronage of the Audley family saw the abbey through to more prosperous times in the 15th century. Upon her death in 1400, Elizabeth, widow of Nicholas III, left £266 13s. 4d. for the purchase of land. She left a further £2 to each monk to pray for the souls of herself and her late husband.[6]

Henry of Audley was a prosperous magnate owing allegiance to Ranulph de Bevill, Earl of

14 Images of the re-enactment of the Battle of Blore Heath at which Lord Audley lost his life.

Chester. He was the great great great grandson of Richard of Toeni, the Conqueror's standard bearer who had ridden at the right hand side of William at the Battle of Hastings.[7] Audley's principal residence was Heleigh, where he was empowered to build a castle. He also had a castle at Redcastle in Shropshire and was responsible for a number of castles on the Welsh borders. His relationship with the Earl of Chester was sufficiently strong to win him favour with the king and upon the death of the earl in 1232, in whose memory Audley granted the abbey the manor of Mixon and Bradnop, Audley became the monarch's chief agent in Cheshire. He was awarded the responsibility for Beeston and Chester castles as well as that at Newcastle-under-Lyme. Despite his extraordinary role in national politics, Audley maintained an active interest in his establishment at Hulton up until his death in 1246, taking part in arbitration sessions settling disputes over land. James, his immediate heir, was a minor when he inherited his father's position. James was a hero of the Battle of Poitiers in 1356 and remained a faithful servant of the Black Prince and Edward III. He was heavily involved in national politics, and spent much time away in the Welsh Marches and in Ireland as well as serving the king in France and Spain. His allegiances brought the family power and prestige; in 1348 James had been created one of the first Knights of the Most Noble Order of the Garter.

Nicholas, the 3rd Baron, died without children and the title passed down the female line. Through this the name Touchet became associated with the barony. The 5th Lord Audley, James Touchet, formed an alliance with the Lancastrian claim to the throne and at the insistence of Queen Margaret raised an army of 10,000 men to stop the Yorkist army of the Earl of Salisbury. This was a huge number of men – the population of London at this time has been estimated at 50,000. Margaret ordered Audley to intercept the Yorkist force of 7,000. The armies met at Blore Heath near Market Drayton on 23 September 1459. It was one of the bloodiest encounters of the Wars of the Roses and resulted in the routing of the Lancastrian force. Audley was one of the estimated 2,400 dead. The Yorkists lost about 56. It marked the beginning of a period in which the Audley family lost influence. The 6th Lord Audley was executed at Tower Hill on 28 June 1497 for his part in the Cornish insurrection and his titles were forfeited. In 1597 the family sold their manorial rights to the lawyer and industrialist Gilbert Gerard of Gerards Bromley.

The abbey was like an Audley family mausoleum. The wills of individuals laid down certain practices for the burial of their bodies. These funerals would have been magnificent occasions and always included sums of money to be given to the poor and to the monks to pray for the soul of the deceased. Excavated remains have revealed a mix of adults and children. The poor dental condition reflects a carbohydrate diet only the rich could have afforded. Perhaps the most significant burial would have been that of Sir William of Audley who was savagely killed on service with King Edward I's army on Anglesey in 1282. His mutilated remains would have been brought back for burial and a skeleton displaying injuries consistent with a violent death has been excavated.[8] A burial found in the chancel was wrapped in rushes and was perhaps the victim of the plague. It is known that James Audley II suffered poor health in later years due to his ceaseless campaigning in France as a young man. He was absolved of attending parliament on health grounds. A skeleton displaying severe arthritis of the spine, arms, hands and feet has been excavated from the site.[9] What is thought to be Elizabeth's skeleton was excavated from before the high altar. Her coffin contained a long hazel wood staff, the sign of a pilgrim. Up to twelve graves containing wands have been found at Hulton. Several of these contained more than one wand. Unlike those found at other burial sites around the country, the wands at Hulton would have been from freshly cut wood, and any in reasonable condition still had their bark. The wands were found in both male and female, adult and adolescent interments. The reason for this grave good is not known. It is possible, like the larger staff of Elizabeth's grave, the wands represented pilgrimage and multiple examples in the grave indicate the number of pilgrimages undertaken by the deceased. It has been suggested that the wand is a meteyard or measure, but their crooked and rough nature seems to preclude this hypothesis.[10]

Rumour and speculation about the early saints are rife, and stories of St Werburgh's local connections are as true in Trentham as they might be elsewhere in the country. Werburgh was niece to King Ethelred. She established a series of nunneries including one at Trentham, or Trichingham as the area was anciently known, and lived an extremely pious life. She died at Trentham in about 699 and expressed a desire to be buried at Hanbury, where her body was laid to rest. Several miracles were claimed at her shrine. During the Danish invasions in Mercia it was decided to remove the body to Chester for safekeeping. On opening the tomb, it is claimed, her remains were incorrupt. They dissolved upon disinterment so that the Danes would not defile the body. The abbey at Chester is dedicated to St Werburgh although the saint's relics were lost after the Reformation. It is claimed that before removal to Hanbury, Werburgh's body was laid to rest at Trentham and the stone

cross in the churchyard is traditionally taken to mark the resting place. It is unlikely this cross is in its original position, since the excavated remains of earlier buildings in the churchyard are at least 13 inches below the present ground level.

Trentham is recorded in Domesday and there is a rare reference to a reeve, or king's representative. This is taken to prove the importance of Trentham, perhaps due to links with a niece of a king. This importance was echoed in the 12th century when a papal bull of Pope Alexander mentioned Henry I as the donor of land to the Priory. There is no reference to a church in Domesday, however, although a priest is mentioned. A nunnery dedicated to St Werburgh, and possibly the one established by the saint herself, was granted to Hugh Lupus, who had been made first Earl of Chester by William in 1069. Hugh Lupus, or Hugh de Avranches to give him his correct name, was one of the Conqueror's most trusted henchmen. He was powerful and ruthless, travelling with a small army rather than a household. Under his influence, the earldom operated almost as an independent unit. He established the Augustinian priory, presumably on the site of the by then decayed nunnery.

On 25 November 1120 a ship carrying William, son and heir to Henry I, sank off Barfleur on its way from Normandy to England. William died, throwing open the question of succession. A number of the English barons recognised Henry's daughter Matilda (also known as Maud) as their future queen in 1127. But, confident that the weaknesses of Stephen of Blois would allow them more power, a strong contingent of the barons supported him when he took the throne in 1135 on the death of Henry. His claim to the throne was through his mother, Adela, daughter of William I. Matilda invaded in 1139 and established a stronghold in the West Country. She exercised royal prerogative over Trentham when she attended a synod held at Lichfield in the same year. During the civil war Stephen was captured in 1141 and Matilda was recognised as queen. She imposed on the barons the taxes they had avoided under Stephen, but with the release of the Conqueror's nephew in 1142 her position was severely weakened. In 1148 she left for Normandy, never to return. Her son Henry married Eleanor of Aquitaine in 1152 and in the following year he returned to England. As heir to the Duke of Aquitaine his possessions were already much larger than England. His army could not decisively beat that of the barons in England, but at Wallingford in Oxfordshire he was able to force the English to end the civil war on his terms. Stephen, the last Norman king, recognised Henry as his heir. In 1154, on the death of Stephen, Henry became the first Plantagenet monarch.

Ranulph de Gervons, 4th Earl of Chester, had remained loyal to Matilda and her son. In return for his loyalty he received large parts of Staffordshire and Henry granted four charters favouring Trentham. In addition he granted them all the woodlands in the manor plus large tracts of marshland to be drained as meadow. The canons also benefited from royal protection. In 1152 Ranulph granted the priory more lands in Trentham in return for the canons praying for his soul. He died the following year, by which time a restoration of the buildings was probably complete. A statue of a knight was discovered during excavations in 1858, believed to be an effigy of Ranulph.[11]

Allegiance to secular leaders was not the only bond the feudal knights observed. We have seen the investment in establishing religious houses and from 1095 men from all ranks of society answered the call of the Church to fight in the crusades in the Middle East. In north Staffordshire records are few and evidence is anecdotal but interesting. The Knights Templar established a community at Keele. The Cistercians had strong links with the Knights Templar and it is possible that Hulton Abbey gave pasture rights to the order on Biddulph Moor. The Knights built the original church at Keele that has since been replaced by a Georgian structure and more recently by the Victorian edifice of 1868-70. The church at Biddulph claims a link with the crusaders too, and in particular the Knights Templar. This claim is largely based on the presence of several stone coffin lids carved with a cross and sword regarded as a symbol of the crusaders. Between 1189 and 1192 Richard I led the Third Crusade accompanied by Ormus de Guidon, or Orm of Biddulph. It is thought that Orm was a Knight Templar. A tradition has it that Orm, son of Richard the Forester, returned from the crusade with a number of Saracen prisoners who were employed as stonemasons. Orm is said to have founded St Chad's Church in Stafford where a Latin inscription on a capital reads, 'ORM VOCATUR QUE ME CONDIDIT' (The man who founded me is called Orm). Various motifs within the church are ascribed as Moorish in influence. At the neighbouring church of St Mary's there is a font that is reputedly originally from St Chad's, the latter being an older church than St Mary's. The font is older then than the church in which it stands and there are claims that it was brought from the Middle East. Many around Biddulph believe the Saracens' descendants still live in the area of Biddulph Moor, having taken the name Bailey. The tradition suggests that the original stonemasons also acted as bailiffs for the Biddulph estate. The modern community was the subject of an article in the *Transactions of the North Staffordshire Field Club* in 1909.

15   These gravestones at Biddulph's St Lawrence's Church are reputedly those of Knights Templar. Some clearly show signs of crosses similar to those worn by Crusaders. The incisions also depict several varieties of weapons and are rather crudely executed. Pevsner assumes them to be monuments to the Knipersley family.

16   Excavations at the Lawn Farm site, part of the Berryhill dig.

During the Middle Ages a buoyant economy stimulated expansion of farming to supply the growing population in towns such as Newcastle. By the middle of the 14th century, 45 north Staffordshire places had markets and half of these had become boroughs.[12] There is little surviving evidence for the quality of housing, especially of the poorer classes from this period in north Staffordshire. John Leland visited the county in 1540 and commented on the timbered housing he saw in such abundance at Tamworth. There is no reason to assume that the other towns and villages were not the same.

Recent excavations at Berryhill Fields have provided evidence of the quality of life in a wealthier bracket of society. A medieval moated site has been known about for some time although the name of the manor has remained unknown. The main residence was excavated in 2000 and comprised a hall with a cross wing at one end.[13] As was commonly the case, the main hall would have been the focus of social life where the administration of the manor was carried out. The lord's private quarters, the cross wing, were accessed via the raised dais at one end of the hall. The hall was built of stone, as this building material was in abundance, although the stone was laid in irregular courses. The archaeologists have found no trace of glass on the site, indicating that the windows were shuttered. Lords were entitled to build dovecotes close to their manor house. Whilst the birds were a readily available source of meat at a time when it was difficult to keep meat over the winter, their droppings were also a rich source of manure. They were also used in the manufacture of gunpowder. A dovecote stood on the site at Berryhill indicating that the lord had some considerable wealth, as the birds were expensive to buy and keep. This was also true of fishponds, evidence for which has also been found. The fish were an important part of the diet at a time when religious observance forbade the eating of meat on certain days. Typically, the ponds would have been stocked with pike, bream, eel, perch and tench. There is also evidence to suggest a deer park was kept near to the site.

The manor had its own arable farming. Ovens found on the site were probably used for malting, drying and smoking meat including fish. Samples of oats and barley have been found in these ovens. The fuel varied according to what the oven was being used for. Straw was used when malting as it added to the flavour of the drink, but wood, charcoal and peat would also have been used. Between the 13th and 15th centuries the site at Berryfields was obviously of some importance. Pottery recovered from the site substantiates this, as do the building materials of the house itself. There is evidence in the field names of the area to suggest the site may have been a hunting lodge for the manor of Fenton.[14] The site was abandoned sometime during the 15th century, perhaps because of the population decline and a series of crop failures following climatic changes.

Little is known about the population figures for the townships that were eventually to make up the modern conurbation, but the population of Newcastle-under-Lyme was about fifty inhabitants plus women and those exempt from taxes on moveable goods.[15] The Black Death also resulted in a movement of population away from upland areas. The plague first reached the county in 1349 and, with a second visitation in 1361, reduced the county's population to an estimated 35,000.[16] Many of the 100 settlements in the county known to have been deserted between 1086 and 1800 are now thought to have been abandoned during the 14th century.[17]

In the aftermath of plague survivors often took over untended arable land. Where labour was in short supply such land was turned over to pasture, with sheep being favoured over cattle in upland areas. Wool became an important commodity in the county. Both Hulton Abbey and Trentham Priory derived much of their income from it and the two houses frequently clashed over grazing rights. James Leveson, who bought the priory in 1540, had made his fortune as a wool merchant. Leveson also briefly owned Hulton Abbey and had bought Lilleshall Abbey before Trentham.

The medieval period saw an increase in church building and restoration. St John the Baptist in Burslem is now largely an 18th-century structure attached to a much earlier western tower. The Church of St Peter ad Vincula was rebuilt in 1826-29, replacing a church possibly built in about 1150 that had replaced an earlier wooden structure. Piers, responds and arches from this medieval building were re-erected in the church-yard in 1887. Parts of St Giles in Newcastle reputedly dated from 1290 are incorporated into the 19th-century rebuilding. The building history of these churches is, like so much in the area at this period, vague, but this is no reason to assume that the inhabitants did not seek to improve their religious buildings. Lichfield Cathedral was, after all, complete by about 1400.

The staple industries of the region also began to develop during this period. There is acutely little evidence of the growth of the ceramic industry and the wares that have been recovered lack inspiration and quality. The industry was still a domestic sideline, with local clays being thrown and fired in small scale kilns such as those excavated at Sneyd Green. Here there were two kilns with radiating fireboxes. The main domed body of the kilns would have been of clay and turf with a central vent. Vessels retrieved from the site included a number of domestic items: jugs, bowls, cooking pots and storage vessels. In 1348 one William the Potter was licensed to make earthenware pots in the area upon payment of 6d. to the lord of the manor. This is an early example of the development of the industry which has only been rivalled by the Roman kiln at Trent Vale and the recently excavated site at the Burslem School of Art, the site of a waste tip containing material from the late 15th to early 18th centuries. Large quantities of Cistercian ware (a brown glazed earthenware made from clay rich in irons and used in a variety of domestic vessels) and white ware (another earthenware used in domestic vessels made from white-firing clays with low levels of iron) have been recovered from this site.

Apart from evidence of coal mining at Holditch from as early as the 2nd century, it is not until the medieval period that we find much to support the development of the industry. The county was still heavily covered with woodland, an obvious source of fuel for small scale pottery and iron working industries. As the woodland was cleared for farming and colonisation, and the demand for fuel increased, the woodlands came under serious pressure and alternative sources of fuel were sought. Biddulph is recorded in Domesday as 'Bidolf', a term meaning a place by a mine. By about 1200 there was an iron mine near Cheadle. Coal was being mined at Tunstall by 1282, Shelton by 1297, Norton-in-the-Moors by 1316 and at Keele by 1333.[18] Drift mining or shallow excavation using bell pits would have left their mark on the landscape, but these have been removed by successive centuries of industrial growth and despoliation. These early mines were small-scale enterprises, probably to feed domestic demand as much as that from pottery kilns. The pits were shallow, the miner descending to the coal face by a rope and undercutting the coal until the roof of the chamber formed was in danger of collapse. The pit was then abandoned and the miners moved further along the seam of coal.

Iron ore was being mined in the Tunstall area by the 13th century and in the Longton, Knutton, Chesterton and Talke areas by the following century. Newcastle appears to have been the centre for buying and selling the ore as the name Ironmarket indicates. These furnaces would have been small-scale enterprises serving a very local market with frying pans, domestic vessels and nails. The size and location of the furnaces changed with the introduction of the blast furnace to this country in the 15th century. These furnaces were often water-powered and hence located by the riverside. During the 17th century the industry experienced a recession because of the shortage of wood fuel but once coke smelting was discovered, and the abundance of coal in the north Staffordshire fields was established, the industry boomed once more. By 1623 there were already complaints of noise as well as atmospheric pollution.[19]

The roads remained in poor condition throughout the medieval period. Potters, it is claimed, dug clay from the roads to use in their wares, leaving large 'potholes' on the surface, an offence for which severe fines were imposed after 1604. Although in a state of decay, the Roman roads were still in use. Everything else depended on ancient trackways and for the most part these were used for moving livestock. As Chester and Carlisle became the major destinations for people travelling north, a new route emerged between Coventry, Stone and Newcastle superseding Watling Street. A second major route, The Earlsway, linked the Cheshire estates of the earls of Chester with their holdings in north Staffordshire and beyond in Nottingham and Leicester.

Three

Secular Growth and Civil Strife

The religious houses continued to dominate the local economy and society throughout the 13th and 14th centuries. By 1307 there were only eight brethren at Trentham Priory when the prior was put on trial for forcibly carrying off corn belonging to Geoffrey Griffin of Clayton. In 1309 Edward II ordered the priory to supply grain, four oxen and 30 sheep in provisions for the king's army fighting in Scotland. The priory's influence grew as the route between the south of the country and Chester and Carlisle developed. In recognition of the hospitality it extended to pilgrims travelling to Canterbury, Henry VI granted further lands from Kingswood to Northwood. By 1516 the prior had a personal income of about £100 per annum. When the Priory was dissolved in 1536 it possessed lands in Trentham, Blurton, Cocknage, Hanchurch, Newstead, Longton, Chorlton, Clayton, Whitmore, Meaford, Seabridge and elsewhere. Prior Thomas Bradwell was granted an annuity of £16 and became the rector of Trentham. Of the other seven canons living at Trentham at the Dissolution, one became rector at Stoke, the remainder moving away.[1]

The *Valor ecclesiasticus* is now generally taken to be an underestimate of the worth of the religious houses on the eve of the Dissolution. Hulton Abbey was valued at £76 14s. 10d.; only two other Cistercian houses were listed with lower incomes. Locally, only the preceptory of the Knights of St John at Keele had a lower income.[2] Crown administrators realised an income of over £107 only a year later. The size of the community at Hulton varied. The regulations of the order required a minimum of 25 upon the foundation of a new monastery. The provision of more land in return for 13 monks saying prayers for the soul of Ranulph of Chester after his death in 1232 would have been observed. A poll tax return for 1377 noted the existence of an abbot and four monks. Upon dissolution there were nine monks including Edward Wilkins, the abbot. On surrender Wilkins received a pension of £20 per annum, a low figure compared with the £26 received by Thomas Chawner, Abbot of Croxden, and the £60 given to Thomas Whitney of Dieulacres. It has been argued that the pension received was not based on the size of the suppressed community, but on the influence of friends of the head of the house and the degree of co-operation with the commissioners.[3] Ordinary members of the community received a pension that would, at £5 if fortunate, keep them above the breadline. These pensions were payable until the former monks obtained employment or until death. The assets of Hulton Abbey were still being disposed of in 1547 when William Ford was appointed as a King's Commissioner for Church Goods and made responsible for the former abbey's assets.

Secular houses were also featuring prominently both in terms of socio-economic

17 The old church in Stoke.

relationships and as physical entities in the landscape. We have already seen the importance of a manor house or hunting lodge at Berryhill. In 1412 land at Smallthorne was granted to the Ford family, moorland farmers from Tittesworth who had settled in the Norton-in-the-Moors area around 1307. In 1580 William Ford began to build Ford Green Hall. He employed Ralph Sutton as master builder for his work at Little Moreton Hall in Cheshire. Ford Green Hall is on a much smaller scale, suited to the status of a yeoman. The complex included a dovecote, however, indicating a certain level of prosperity, as well as stables with labourers' quarters above and

barns. The grounds included orchards and a vegetable garden. The Hall itself is timber framed. Stone was still too expensive for the yeoman farmer to use.

The Tudor and Stuart periods witnessed a continuation of secular rebuilding on a scale not seen before. In the county of Stafford-shire there were no new churches between the reformation and 1600.[4] Yeoman farmers such as the Fords at Smallthorne built their timber-framed houses, a method of construction that remained in favour in this class and in lowland areas until well into the 1600s, though by then the framing was no longer purely structural but more decorative.

Although brick had been used in Lichfield as early as the 1490s, widespread usage was not adopted until much later in the 17th century. Larger land magnates were able to take on the former monastic estates. At Keele, the Sneyd family bought the preceptory and in 1580 built a mansion on the estates. This set a precedent whereby the family chose to live some distance away from their tenants, building the house in its own park. At the other extreme, at Great Sandon, the village was pulled down and rebuilt away from the manor house and the land formerly occupied by the village was emparked. By the middle of the 17th century there were nearly eighty parks in the county, many of which were stocked with deer.

James Leveson, owner of Lilleshall Abbey, bought Trentham Priory in 1540.[5] Leveson also bought Rushton Grange from the sale of estates formerly belonging to Hulton Abbey in 1539, quickly re-selling it to Richard Biddulph for £130 7s. 0d.[6] The Leveson family continued to live at Lilleshall until settling at Trentham in 1630. During the time they spent at Trentham before moving there permanently, they would presumably have lived in the former abbot's residence. At Biddulph, Francis Biddulph built an impressive stone hall, now ruinous. Pilasters on the entrance range date from about 1589. The mansion was sacked during the Civil War, when it was subjected to heavy cannon fire.

The action against Biddulph Old Hall was perhaps one of the most significant events of the English Civil War in north Staffordshire. The Biddulph family were Catholic supporters of Charles I in an area that supported the Parliamentarian cause. When the Parliamentarians won over Cheshire, in 1644, the Catholic Brereton family sought refuge at Biddulph. The Parliamentarians, under the command of another member of the Brereton family, laid siege to the Hall with its contingent of 150 troops. Heavy artillery was used against the buildings and the families inside were left with no alternative but to surrender. The remainder of the Hall was plundered by the local population, leaving only a romantic ruin today. Elsewhere in the county, Stafford Castle, Tutbury Castle and Eccleshall Castle were all partially destroyed by the Parliamentarian forces.

There are no surviving houses of the lower classes. Plot noted in his *Natural History of Staffordshire* published in 1686 that their houses tended to be turf-roofed. The walls were presumably cob. Peat would have been the main fuel for the fire. In Burslem he noted the thatched cottages surrounded by their own hedged and enclosed plots of land or tofts on which the cottager would grow beans, peas and other vegetables. They may also have kept pigs or hens. At Kinver houses were carved out of the sandstone outcrops and some continued in use until the 20th century. The poor quality of housing certainly helped the spread of disease and infection. In Burslem in 1647 there was an outbreak of plague, the severity of which was not recorded in the parish registers. It would seem the epidemic broke out in the Rushton Grange area. At Hot Lane, where living conditions were particularly poor, most of the community disappeared. Although it cannot be proved beyond certainty, it is thought the plague was introduced through rat fleas in clothing brought from London by an Italian governess to the Biddulph family. Undoubtedly the family was still held in suspicion following the Civil War siege. The woman was known for her vocal skills and was one of the first to perish. The Biddulph family was ostracised and ruined as several members died of the plague. Burial of the bodies in the churchyard was not allowed for fear of infection, and the mass burial plot where they were laid to rest was known as 'Singing Kate's Hole' after the governess.[7] Francis Biddulph left soon after for London with his one surviving son. The people had little with which to fight the plague. Even as late as 1683 one remedy was to

> Take Fetherfew [feverfew], Matfellon, Mugwort, Sweet Scabi'us mathes [grubs, maggots] of each a like quantity and stamp em and temper em with Stale Ale and give *the* sick to drink six spoonfuls at once, and it shall save *the* man or woman.[8]

Plot also noted the agricultural practices of the county. Drawing a line through the county along the River Trent, he placed pasture and dairy farming in the north east and moorland areas. He noted that the cheese and butter produced in this region was of sufficiently high quality to attract dealers from London. Cheese was sold by weight, but the butter was sold in 14lb. cylindrical pots made at Burslem.

Farming was largely pastoral. Livestock was moved between upland and lowland pastures and preference was given to cattle over sheep. Enclosure of open fields had been gradually taking place since the reign of Henry VIII. The open fields of Tunstall were enclosed in 1614. By the late 17th century writers such as Celia Fiennes were noting the quantity of enclosures around the county. Land was being brought under cultivation through woodland clearance and use of former waste. Frequent flooding by the county's major rivers improved the fertility of meadowland.

Arable farming was carried out in the north east region identified by Plot; it was not an exclusively pastoral area. The open field system was practised and some of these fields were not enclosed until the 19th century. In Penkhull the farm buildings were either on or adjacent to the high street and each had a toft. The farmers had a number of strips of land of about an acre in each of the three open fields. In addition they had grazing rights on the wasteland. In Penkhull the wasteland, or common, lay at what was to become the centre of the modern village, where the church now stands.[9] Under this system of farming, where everybody had their share of rich and poor land, level and rough land, flooded or well-drained land, co-operation was important but it restricted innovation and enterprise. During the 16th century the field systems seen today around the Berryhill Fields area were established. Thomas Essex sold much of his land interests to local yeomen between 1565 and 1612 and these farmers also supplemented their incomes through small scale industry such as the emergent craft of pottery making, spinning and weaving and butter and cheese making.[10] But it was glass making that emerged first as a major industry in the county. The necessary natural ingredients of clay, sand and timber were in abundance and attracted glass makers of the highest order from France. The county was second only to the Weald.

Surviving wills and inventories for the period indicate the wealth and lifestyles enjoyed by these families. Personal fortunes range from £24 to £324 with an income of £75 being considered modest.[11] Farms are listed as having cattle, pigs, poultry and horses, tools for working the land, as well as crops such as corn and hay. Large iron domestic items are also listed in these inventories. A comparative study of inventories of farms in the Adderley area of neighbouring Shropshire from the 17th and 18th centuries shows how important cheese was to the local economy and is again a measure of the wealth of the yeoman class in the north Midlands. Richard

Furber, who had an exceptionally large herd, had £168 worth of cheese (which amounts to about 8 tons!) in 1660. William Tankard who had fifty cows had four tons valued at £80 in 1695. Between 1660 and 1750 seventeen farmers died leaving cheese stocks of about one ton valued at over £20.

Pottery emerged as the staple cottage industry in the northern part of Staffordshire during the Tudor and Stuart period. In 1603 a dish maker called Gervase Griffye is listed in Tunstall. In the same town in 1635 three men appeared before the manor court accused of digging clay from the highways and waste land.[12] Pottery was being made at Penkhull by about 1600 and there are records of butterpots being made in Stoke by the end of the century, concurrent with their manufacture in Hanley. Shelton clay was being used to make clay pipes in Newcastle. Fenton and Longton developed an industry later than did the more northern towns. By the time of Plot's itinerary through the county Burslem had asserted itself as the mother town, and Plot commented that the finest pottery made in the area came from there. The potters lived in small cottages in their own area of enclosed land. The enclosure contained bottle-shaped ovens. The farmer was becoming a potter as demand for domestic vessels and clay pipes increased.

Four

Urbanisation and Industrial Revolution

During the mid-17th century many of the larger houses in the county were altered or rebuilt. As the yeoman classes continued to build in wood, the gentry and aristocracy adopted brick and stone on a scale not seen before. At Whitmore the timber-framed building was encased in a brick shell in 1676.[1] The hall is connected with the churchyard by an avenue of trees with a ha-ha near to the church that was also rebuilt at about the same time. At Caverswall the castle was adapted as a house in about 1615. The crenellations were replaced by balustradings. At Trentham the ecclesiastical buildings were demolished and a new residence built for the Leveson family who moved their seat to the site in 1630. The Hall designed by Francis Smith resembled the Queen's Palace in St James's Park and was extended between 1768 and 1778 by Capability Brown and Henry Holland. Brown also landscaped the grounds and included a large lake that dominates the park today. Also prominent in the park is a monument to the 1st Duke of Sutherland. The column was built in 1830 and atop it is a huge bronze statue of the duke. Attached to the estate but now separated from it by the busy A34 is a huge monolithic mausoleum built in 1808 to the design of Charles Heathcote Tatham. It is the only Grade I listed building in Stoke and is a Greek cross in plan with ashlar wall sloping inwards towards the top. In preparation for the Leveson-Gower's move away from Trentham, the bodies of family members buried in the catacombs were removed to other sites in the cemetery and re-buried in lead lined coffins. At one point the deterioration of the building placed it on the most-at-risk list and in 2000 it required at least £250,000 maintenance work.

18 The avenue leading from the church of St Mary and All Saints to Whitmore Hall. The south front of the hall, facing the church, is of 1676.

19 St John's Church in Burslem. The 18th-century nave and chancel adjoin a much earlier tower.

It was during the late 18th and early 19th centuries that the scattered villages and hamlets began to merge and develop. Burslem, Penkhull and Hanley were perhaps the only ones recognisable as villages of any size. The area suffers from the lack of any maps for the period although there are the descriptions written by Plot, Leland and Fiennes. An early 18th-century illustration of Burslem shows a clustering of houses and a large number of potbanks set aside from the parish church. Penkhull focused on its central common, over which the villagers had grazing rights; the village church was some distance away at Stoke, which did not develop as a village or town until the arrival of the turnpike roads and the Trent and Mersey Canal in the 18th century.[2]

Hanley was in effect two villages or hamlets roughly half a mile apart. The centre of one settlement was at what is now the junction of Keelings Lane and Town Road; the other centre was Lower Green, now the market. By the mid-16th century the area was known as Hanley Green. As the town grew to include Shelton, the parish church of St John's was built in 1738. The church was extended within thirty years and was rebuilt in 1788-90.

Described in 1795 as the 'pleasantest village in the pottery',[3] Tunstall had about one hundred acres of land contained within six open

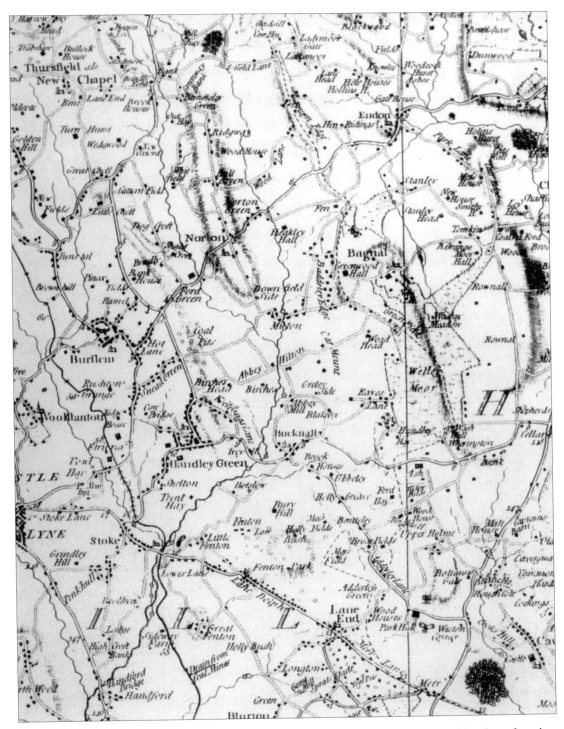

20 Detail from the map of 1775 by Yates showing the distribution of the villages and hamlets of north Staffordshire. One of the earliest maps for the area appeared in Plot's *The Natural History of Staffordshire*.

fields in the 16th century. These were enclosed in 1614.[4] By the time of the 1666 Hearth Tax, there were 17 households liable to pay it. The neighbouring village of Goldenhill, which was to develop an iron industry along with the likes of Apedale and Silverdale, existed by 1670 and by 1775 was almost as large as Tunstall. By the time of the cutting of the Trent and Mersey Canal, Goldenhill was also a noted mining community.

The 1666 Hearth Tax returns list 17 people in Fenton Vivian and 16 in Fenton Culvert liable to pay the tax.[5] By 1775 there were three centres of population. Lower Lane and Lane Delph were the most populous and lay

21 St Peter ad Vincula, the parish church of Stoke, built between 1826 and 1829 a short distance from the site of the earlier church it replaced.

22 The church of St Thomas at Penkhull was completed in 1843. It was built on land once used for common grazing.

23   Etruria Hall in an idyllic, rural setting in the late 18th century.

along the main Newcastle to Uttoxeter road. Lane End and Longton covered about 1,000 acres. Lane End developed during the 17th century as a result of mining and iron working. In 1666 there were 13 houses in Longton and 12 in Lane End. The growth of Lane End is reflected in the provision of a church in 1762 and a school the following year. A market square was built in 1789 in an area now covered by Times Square. The name of Lane End was officially changed to Longton in the 19th century.

To a large extent it was the roads that influenced the development of the Six Towns as a sprawling, linear conurbation. Housing tended to be along the line of the roads. There was no planning: houses were simply built to demand on available spare land. With the exceptions of Tunstall and Stoke, the towns were noted for their irregularity. Demand came from the owners of the growing potbanks and mines who sought to house their workers within easy travelling distance of work. Up until the 17th century, and in some areas

24 The intricate network of roads around Burslem can be seen clearly in this detail from the Yates map of 1775.

beyond, the roads were merely tracks that connected small villages and hamlets. As the pottery industry developed, raw materials from outside the locality were brought in by pack-horse. Finished vessels were taken from the potters in the same manner, and the condition of the roads resulted in many broken pots. As the volume of raw materials and products increased carts were used, but these simply could not pass along the roads in the area. After their introduction in 1673 stagecoaches also served the region, and the London to Carlisle road was one of the busiest in the

country. These coaches travelled up to thirty miles a day in the winter, perhaps double that figure in the summer. They were severely hampered by poor conditions. Timetables often carried the disclaimer, 'If God permit.' The Lichfield coaches that started running in 1751 took four days to reach London. The itinerary of the Uttoxeter coaches to London brought them through Lane End, Stoke, Penkhull, Hanley Green, Burslem and Tunstall. They ran from Uttoxeter every Monday and Thursday, returning on Wednesdays and Saturdays.

The canals also influenced the nature of the towns. The first canal, the Grand Trunk or Trent and Mersey, was engineered by James Brindley. Josiah Wedgwood cut the first clod on 26 July 1766. The cutting took on the air of a great ceremony, with other local notables taking their turn with the shovel. A sheep was roasted whole in Burslem market place to mark the event.

Before the coming of the canal, the region was landlocked. The River Trent was too shallow to navigate; access to navigable rivers was at Winsford in Cheshire, for a route to Liverpool and the Americas, and at Willington in Derbyshire for the River Humber to Europe. It was apparent to the entrepreneurial potters that in order to develop and exploit national and international markets this situation had to change. Even the short packhorse journey between the potbanks and Winsford or Willington resulted in too many breakages, was costly and took too long. Schemes to link the Trent and the Mersey were discussed as early as 1717 but surveying work did not begin until 1758, when the grand idea was to link the Trent, Mersey, Severn and Thames rivers with a system of canals. Josiah Wedgwood, Earl Gower and John Sneyd, along with the Duke of Bridgewater, Thomas Anson, Matthew Boulton, and Samuel Garbett, arguably the most powerful

25   The Wedgwood Works at Etruria.

industrialists at the time, were instrumental in bringing what was to become the Trent and Mersey Canal through the Potteries region.

The canal was a major engineering accomplishment by Brindley. He had cut the world's first deadwater canal for the Duke of Bridgewater between 1759 and 1761 for the transport of the duke's coal from his collieries at Worsley to Manchester. From the start of work the major obstacle to the canal's success was the Harecastle Tunnel between Kidsgrove and Tunstall. At 2,880 yards it was the largest civil engineering project in Britain and work on it commenced immediately after the ceremonial sod cutting by Wedgwood. On completion of the canal in 1777 the tunnel was described as the eighth wonder of the world, but Brindley was dead. Wedgwood

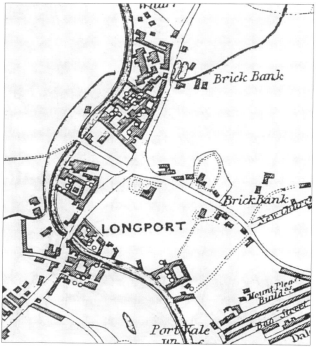

26 Wedgwood's Etruria Works was designed as a rural factory intended to offer better working conditions.

27 Detail of Longport from the 1832 map by Hargreaves.

opened his Etruria Works on the banks of the canal, significantly at the point at which the Leek and Newcastle turnpike road crosses the canal. From 1773 further factories were built along the line of the canal, particularly around the area to become known as Longport, formerly known as Longbridge, a small collection of cottages. John Brindley, younger brother of the canal's engineer, built the first factories. It was here that the Davenports established their business in 1794, to which they added their glass making operations after 1801. Nineteenth-century factories at Middleport and Newport were later to be swallowed by Burslem.[6]

28   The two entrances to the Harecastle tunnels. Brindley's original tunnel lies unused in the background whilst that of Thomas Telford on the left features a towpath.

The canal was a major success, so much so that the Harecastle Tunnel soon became a bottleneck and Thomas Telford was commissioned to build a second that was opened in April 1827. At 2,926 yards, Telford's tunnel was longer than that of Brindley's. It also had the advantage over Brindley's tunnel of having a towpath. In the original tunnel, the bargees had to 'leg it', by lying on their backs and pushing the boat along with their feet on the roof of the tunnel. Brindley's original tunnel was later to be seriously affected by mining subsidence and closed in 1914.

In order to supply Newcastle with coal, another canal was cut from the town to Chesterton in 1775. As part of the agreement for the canal the maximum price of coal was set at 5s. per ton.[7] The Newcastle-under-Lyme Canal was cut following an Act of Parliament in 1795. A further canal connected this with

29   The Trent and Mersey Canal near the Harecastle Tunnels.

the Newcastle to Chesterton Canal in 1798. Authorised in 1776 and built in 1777 was the Caldon Canal. It was during its construction that Brindley died, on 27 September 1772. The canal stretched from Etruria where it joined the Trent and Mersey Canal to Froghall. A branch to Leek, along with the feeder reservoir, later to be Rudyard Lake, was authorised in 1797. The canal was extended to Uttoxeter by an Act passed in 1797. The canals successfully linked the pottery manufacturers with their markets and with their sources of raw materials. Corn mills were being converted to mills for grinding flint and stone to serve the pottery industry. Transportation costs were reduced significantly too. In 1774 it cost one and a halfpence per ton, down from the ten pence it used to cost.[8] At their peak in 1888 the canals carried 2.2 million tons.

By the 17th century the coal mining industry was well established. Primarily the mines supplied diverse industries such as small metal-based trades, breweries, the Cheshire salt industry, glass making and tile making. Traditionally these industries had made use of wood and charcoal in their processes, but manufacturers were looking for an alternative as wood became more scarce during the century. As the century gave way to the 18th, domestic demand was increasing too. In 1660 Charles II granted a licence to Sir John Bowyer to mine coal in the royal manors north of the River Trent. Thomas Poole was mining coal in Talke from about 1674, realising a profit of some £800.[9]

It was from about 1750, however, that large scale mining began. The reasons for this were the growth in the pottery industry (the opening of the county's first porcelain works in Longton is ascribed to the local availability of coal), the switch to coal in the iron industry and the improved road and canal systems. Many of these early pits were restricted in size and hence output by the risk of flooding, poor ventilation and inadequate winding mechanisms. In order to meet demand, innovation was imperative. Newcomen's atmospheric steam engine, introduced in 1712, was one of many that allowed the mines to be pumped clear of flood water and allowed extraction of coal deeper than the hitherto average shaft of 150 to 200 feet. Previously drainage had depended on the cutting of gutters, and as late as 1820 colliers were still cutting these at the pits at Sneyd, Harecastle and Chatterley. By 1830, however, a depth of 2,000 feet had been reached at Apedale, accessed by an inclined plane and a shaft of some 720 feet. A steam engine was installed underground to haul the coal up the inclined plane.

It was not just the growing urban areas that provided the impetus for industrial growth in north Staffordshire. Although the new entrepreneurs such as Wedgwood played such crucial roles in developing industry in the area, members of the local aristocracy and the gentry continued to play a part until at least the mid 19th-century. Earl Gower (1721-1803) personally risked his fortune by investing in the canal networks and in mineral extraction. He was brother-in-law to the Duke of Bridgewater, and it was Gower who actually employed Brindley to carry out his survey in 1759 for the Trent and Mersey Canal. Gower was, from 1785, the first Marquis of Stafford, and owned lands at Lilleshall in Shropshire from which coal was mined. On his death in 1803 his second son Earl Granville assumed ownership of the companies and developed their interests in Staffordshire. In 1833, the year of his death, the 2nd Marquis of Stafford became the 1st Duke of Sutherland.

In Hanley and Shelton early attempts to create an iron industry had failed. In 1839 the 4th Earl Granville established works near Cobridge Road in an area where he was already mining coal. The 5th Earl established new works at Etruria in 1850 along the canal and created the Shelton Bar Iron Company. At Tunstall the Goldendale works had been established by the Williamson brothers. Longton, late in its development of a ceramic industry, was the scene of several ironworks by the 17th century. Ironstone was being mined at Meir Heath by 1679 and there was a furnace in operation by the middle of the century, operated by a consortium that included Philip Foley and Obadiah Lane.[10] Acquiring mineral rights from the Duke of Sutherland, William Hanbury Sparrow mined ironstone at Lane End, where he also operated a forge. By 1829 the forge was producing 1,367 tons mainly for the south Staffordshire nail making industry, which was perhaps the largest consumer of north Staffordshire iron.[11] Many of these forges were located by canals, the weight of the produce being far too much for other forms of transport available at the time. Exceptions to this were the blast furnaces dating from 1789 at Apedale, operated by Parker's from the south of the county, and at Silverdale (1792). Like many other small forges, these suffered with the recession that followed the end of the Napoleonic Wars in 1815. The recession was only truly reversed in 1829 with the invention of the blast furnace. Granville's works at Shelton incorporated three blast furnaces. Apedale was rebuilt to accommodate blast furnaces in 1840.

As industry adopted the factory system it required larger numbers of employees living closer to hand. Higher wages enticed people from the rural areas in to the new industrial

30 A view of the canal contrasting the purity of the swans' plumage with the bottle ovens.

and urban areas that were clustered, in the early days of the Industrial Revolution, around the riverbanks and later the coalfields. The population of England, Scotland and Wales rose from seven million in 1700 to nine million by 1800 and to 37 million by 1900. In 1801 the population of the parish of Stoke-on-Trent was 16,414. By 1861 it had risen to 71,308.[12] In the Staffordshire Potteries it was documented that, except in extreme circumstances, families had their own homes. The first issue of the *Sentinel* newspaper in 1854 carried advertisements for houses costing £60 and £70 including the site on which they were built. More typically, people rented their house at anything between 3s. or 4s. a week.[13] In Penkhull 421 people lived in 91 households and in Shelton 497 lived in 100 households, nearly five people per household in effect.

We have already seen that in the north Staffordshire region, like elsewhere in the country, workers' housing developed in a random, unplanned manner. There were exceptions. Josiah Wedgwood proved to have enlightened ideas about the housing and lifestyle of his workers. His factory at Etruria was set in the grounds of his home at Etruria Hall and was built in the style of estate buildings, perhaps a homage to the rural beginnings of industry. The name Etruria is evocative of an area in Italy, the source of a style of pottery Wedgwood emulated. In 1769, the year it opened, the factory employed 120 and this number rose to 150 during its first year of operation.[14] Along the turnpike road that crossed the canal at Wedgwood's factory, he built model houses complete with gardens for his workers. The village he created was an early garden village, albeit incomplete, the church and school only being added at a later date. It was the first industrial village of its kind in the world. The houses were built along one street and had

31 Main entrance to the Wedgwood Institute in Burslem. Built in 1863-9, the Institute's façade features reliefs of the months of the year. The building commemorates one of the city's most famous people and provided educational facilities. William Gladstone laid the foundation stone.

earth floors. According to Warrilow,

> they were roomy and well lit, with quaint windows of small panes of green glass ... The front door steps were of iron, six inches wide, and were always kept beautifully polished ... By 1865 there were approximately one hundred and twenty five numbered, and sixty-five un-numbered houses in the village.[15]

The village also boasted several bakehouses and wells.

Despite the praises lavished on the housing and concept at Etruria, there are few references

32   The Burslem works of Enoch Wood & Sons with a crenellated façade adding an individual touch. Many potbanks remained plain but others added classical influences to their street frontages.

to either in the Wedgwood archives. It would seem, however, that the houses were not particularly different to those built elsewhere in the area. Whilst the quality may have been superior, the ground plan of two up, two down cottages may have been widely used. In older properties one downstairs room with two upstairs have been reported. As is usual, the lower quality housing does not survive as evidence of the workers' lot. Water supply, sewage removal and so on featured little. Coal fires burning in open grates made the houses smoky, resulting in doors often being open, and facilitated the spread of illness, and contributing to higher numbers of chest related diseases.

Terraced housing in Stoke exhibits many fine architectural details executed in terracotta

aimed at attracting rent-paying residents. The quality of houses reflected the market they were aimed at. Stoke-on-Trent has avoided the excesses of back-to-back housing and court developments experienced in other industrial centres but there are contemporary descriptions of some of the worst. In Hanley and Shelton, for instance, houses were built around an oblong filled with walled enclosures in which pigs were kept. In this area, too, were middens and wells.[16]   Ground plans became more elaborate and included such refinements as a lobby or hall, but these internal improvements went hand-in-hand with the loss of other amenities. Early 19th-century housing in the city often had a front garden; some even had a rear garden too. These disappeared as the

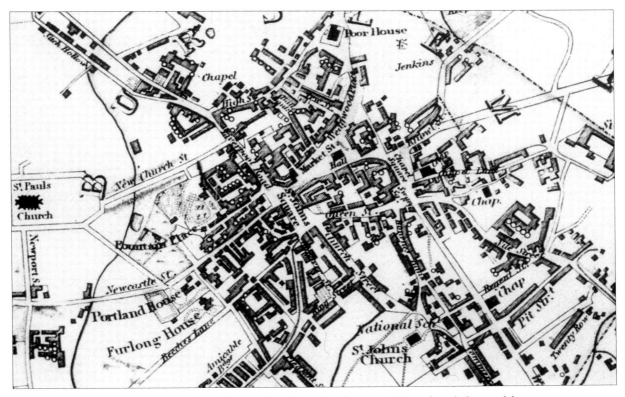

33 The Hargreaves map is detailed enough to show the close proximity of workplace and home.

century progressed, as did the room for vegetable plots as demand rose for space on which to build.

Throughout the 18th century government became more aware of its responsibilities towards the population. No government before the first census in 1801, though had detailed information about the population. Commentators of the period made many claims about the nature of the population growth and the knock-on effect, in terms of costs, of supporting this growth. In 1798 Malthus's *Essay on Population* claimed the population would always exceed the supply of food and that poverty and starvation were natural ways of regulating the numbers, echoing mid-century concerns that the poor married young

and produced large families. This extreme thinking had been modified by 1803, when Malthus argued for moral constraints to control the population, even though as early as 1701 women were waiting until between the ages of 25 and 30 before they married. Men usually married between 25 and 35 years of age despite a tax levied on bachelors between 1694 and 1705. The sustained growth in the 19th-century population was the result in part of the demand for child labour, the greater number of jobs and the improved level of wages and relief payments under the Speenhamland system. These encouraged earlier marriages and larger families in order to gain more income. There was a concurrent drop in the death rate, too, attributed to control of infectious diseases such as smallpox and fewer outbreaks of the plague.

Relief for those in need had been passed down to the parish in 1601. The Act introducing this was a clear statement that relief for the poor was a public concern. Residents of the parish paid a tax to assist orphans and parents unable to support their family, those who were disabled and unable to work, the aged and the unemployed. To relieve the burden in rural parishes, children were often apprenticed to industrialists in the growing towns. Expenditure on poor relief soared during the late 18th and early 19th centuries. In Stoke-on-Trent the cost to the parish in 1776 was £1,006 7s. which had risen to £5,116 5s. by 1803. In Burslem the figures were £385 17s. and £2,141 2s. respectively. In some areas, notably rural ones, the figures fell slightly. In Whitmore the poor relief fell from £60 2s. in 1776 to £59 14s. in 1803, possibly because of migration of labourers to the neighbouring industrial centres in search of work and accommodation.[17] These were also years of high food prices caused by the Napoleonic Wars and low wages, especially for agricultural labourers, who were forced to move to find better wages to support their families or else seek relief in their parish. Anxious to avoid any possibility of a revolution in this country, the authorities introduced the Speenhamland system of relief which guaranteed that those unable to achieve a minimum wage would have the difference made up from the local taxes administered through the vestry. Farmers kept wages down, quick to realise that what they did not pay the parish would.

The Poor Relief Act of 1601 had introduced the idea of the workhouse where able-bodied labourers could be found work. The concept had not worked but it was picked up again in the later 18th century when parishes were allowed to combine resources to operate their own workhouses. The masters and matrons of the workhouses were paid on the number to whom they offered relief and soon it became obvious that it was cheaper to send the older residents of a parish to the workhouse rather than pay for them to continue living at home. Thus was born what became such a feared institution in society. Early workhouses such as those at Norton-in-the-Moors and Cheadle were indistinguishable from other housing; they were very much a part of the community they served. Poverty was not a situation to be ashamed off. By the time of Malthus and the imposing workhouses of Stoke and of Chell, which was known locally as the Bastille, this attitude had disappeared. These larger institutions were deliberately inhospitable and intended to be isolated so the destitute were sent away from their communities. At Cheadle it was suggested that all those in receipt of relief should be forced to wear the letters 'CP' on their clothing to identify them.[18] Confinement to the workhouse was very much a form of social control. Within its walls the inmates were separated from their family members and the other sex. An authoritarian regime denied any individuality. The lowest of the low, the vagrants, were locked in cells and forced to crush stone into graded sizes in order to get food. By 1803 a significant number of the county's parishes were sending their poor to the workhouse, of which there were thirty-nine in 1776.[19]

The original Stoke workhouse stood near Penkhull and was built in 1735. By 1775 there were eighty inmates who were found work in the growing potbanks. It was noted at the time for its cleanliness and the care given to the older people living there:

The workhouse is on an elevated spot and will be inspected with pleasure by the philanthropist for cleanliness and comfort afforded to the aged and infirm, the weak minded and the destitute. In fact all the attentions of humanity are supplied to them.[20]

This workhouse was later sold by the vestry and was demolished only as late as 1967. A new one was built in an isolated position along the London Road near Newcastle on the site of an old leadworks. This institution could house about 500 and cost in excess of £6,000. Its isolation meant that there was no employment for the inmates in close proximity. Instead, work was brought to the workhouse. A wharf was even built so that stone could be brought for the vagrants to crush and then shipped out to the potbanks. An internal struggle to maintain the separation of males and females, young and old, healthy and sick and parents and children was met at Stoke with a programme of new building which included, as government legislation required, school rooms for the children. Eventually a large Elizabethan-style school was built in 1866. Over a period of time the children were to be removed from the workhouse completely and housed at Penkhull.

Similar in scale and intent to the Penkhull institution was the Norton-in-the-Moors workhouse. This was built adjacent to Norton Hall in 1798, an act almost symbolic of the ready acceptance of philanthropic attitudes towards the aged, infirm and poor of the parish. The workhouse was extended in about 1825 and it would appear that the matron and master lived in, sharing the same conditions as the inmates. The inmates were never large in number, fluctuating between ten in 1814 and two in 1815. Typical of the inmates were the unemployed, unmarried mothers, vagrants and the sick. When the workhouse system was reformed into one of unions and guardians, Norton became part of the Leek Union and its inmates were transferred to the Leek workhouse.

By the time of the Trentham workhouse, built in 1809–10, attitudes towards the poor and less fortunate members of society were beginning to change. This workhouse could take about fifty-six inmates, usually children, unmarried mothers, the aged and sick, but unlike Penkhull and Norton, there already existed at Trentham a strict regime of rules bordering on the institutionalisation that was to become synonymous with workhouses. The inmates were encouraged to go out to work and significantly the workhouse was located as close as possible to the growing potbanks in Longton on land donated by the Duke of Sutherland. Under the reforms, Trentham became part of the Stone Union, to which town the inmates were moved.

The Burslem workhouse was enlarged in 1835 probably in an attempt to avoid losing control to a cross-parish institution that was being discussed. The 300 inmates were seen as earners, bringing income to the parish, and their life in the workhouse was little more than institutionalised organisation of cheap labour. A few years earlier two inmates of the Wolstanton workhouse had requested permission to marry and this resulted in a report suggesting this was not to be encouraged and that 'intercourse of the sexes' should be avoided. At Burslem the workhouse was split into two parts to segregate the sexes completely. Despite this, the Burslem and Wolstanton vestries were forced to merge in a Union and a new workhouse was built at Chell. Here too the guardians were obsessed with segregation, to the extent that the venereal wards were given over to accommodation of prostitutes and the iron gates that separated the girls' and boys' yards were taken out and the spaces boarded up.[21]

If there was concern for the physical well being of parishioners, there was also concern for the spiritual. Only seven churches had been

34   The Jubilee Chapel, Tunstall.

built in the whole of Staffordshire between the Reformation and 1800. With the growth of the urban areas new churches were needed, and in large numbers. During the 1820s and 1830s many were built, including 38 Commissioners churches. Bishop Lonsdale (1843-67) consecrated, on average, a new church every eight weeks – 156 in total throughout the county.[22] In addition Catholics and Nonconformists were able to build their own churches and chapels. This had a marked effect on both urban and rural areas.

The Church Commissioners were by and large responsible for the major building programme during the 19th century, but many of the churches would not have been built

had it not been for the benevolence and enterprise of individuals. Christ Church in Fenton is typical of this. It was built at the bequest of one Ralph Bourne who left a £1,000 endowment plus £2,500 towards building costs. This latter figure was augmented with a further £3,000 from his sister. The church was built between 1838-9 and the new parish was created in 1841. It was a gothic building of brick with stone dressings and seated about 1,000 people. Previously Fenton had been a part of the massive parish of Stoke. The present Christ Church replaced it in 1890 seating about 2,000. Christ Church in Tunstall was built in 1832 at a cost of £4,000, of which £1,000 was met by local donations,

35 St John's, Hanley dating from 1790. The earlier structure of 1738 was built at the expense of John Bourne.

36 The Bethesda Chapel, Hanley before closure. The façade of 1859 was added to an earlier building of 1819.

new chapel was built and consecrated as a chapel of ease to Stoke parish church in 1795. St John the Baptist, since demolished, was built around the end of the 18th century in Times Square in a mixture of gothic and contemporary classical influences in the form of Tuscan columns. The Church of St James the Less was built to the designs of James Trubshaw who was also the architect of Stoke's St Peter's. The Duke of Sutherland paid for the Church of the Resurrection in Dresden, a part of Longton, which acted as a chapel of ease for Blurton parish church. It is a red brick building with diapered patterns, described by Pevsner as 'demonstrative' and as an 'architectural mystery'. Inside the brickwork is yellow with red bands. It is claimed the architect was George Gilbert Scott.

Three men, John Bourne, who was the Town Clerk at Newcastle-under-Lyme, Richard Hollins and his father-in-law John Adams, were responsible for the provision of the first church in Hanley. It was a small affair, seating only 400, but in 1764, 26 years after it was built, Bourne had it enlarged. The church became an early victim of mining subsidence in the area and was replaced by a new chapel in 1790.[23] According to Greenslade, subscription and the sale of pews, all of which save eighty were privately owned, covered the cost. St John the Evangelist was built between 1788 and 1790 and is thought to be an early example of a steel framed church.[24] The date plaque in the vestibule refers to an earlier chapel of 1738, not this church. St John's was extended and modernised throughout the 19th century. St Mark's in Shelton was built in 1834 and seats 2,100, making it one of the largest capacity churches in the diocese. Costs were again met for the most part by the Commissioners with some input from public subscriptions. Like many of the Commissioners' churches, it is gothic in style.

the remainder being from the Commissioners. A parish was created in 1837 which was split in 1843 leaving Tunstall as a separate parish to that of Oldcott and Ravenscliffe.

Longton lay within Stoke parish until the 19th century. Public contributions had paid for the construction of a small church in 1762, but its status is unclear. Upon completion it was registered for worship by dissenters, although it seems Anglican services were also held there after its consecration in 1764. A

37 Stafford Street, Longton in about 1910. The Wesleyan Methodist Chapel stands to the left, whilst to the right, below the pawnbroker's sign, can be seen the tower of the Market Hall of 1863.

Undoubtedly it was the Bethesda Chapel that caught the imagination however. Built in 1819 with a façade of 1859, this chapel is huge in its scale and intent. Originally surrounded by streets of terraced housing, the chapel held an impressive 3,000 behind its Italianate frontage. For many it was the home of the Methodist New Connexion. With the death of Wesley in 1791, reform was expected in the Methodist movement. The New

Connexion was founded in 1797 by Alexander Kilham of Hanley after he and several of his supporters, notable pottery manufacturers, were expelled from the Leeds Conference. They agreed to meet in people's houses, but the growing numbers attracted to their beliefs and practices made this an inappropriate solution. A coach house holding 150 people was acquired on Albion Street but this was replaced by a brick building capable of holding 600 in

1798. Methodism had an immediate appeal to the people of the Potteries. Very soon it was the strongest congregation in Hanley. In 1811 the building was extended but demand exceeded the number of rented seats available and further extensions were approved in 1812. The new chapel was opened on 7 May 1820, and with the graveyard and school building formed a complex within the industrial housing provided on roads such as Albion Street, John Street, York Street, Vine Street, Mollart Street, Gloucester Street, Milner Court, George Street, Bethesda Street and Lichfield Street.

But the chapel also attracted the patronage of the Hanley elite. Major pottery families such as the Ridgways and the Meighs played an active role in the business of the chapel and family members were buried in the vast crypt, an unusual feature in a Methodist chapel. These families dominated Hanley during the 19th century. John Ridgway it has been claimed, held every public office a layman could hold from magistrate to Deputy Lieutenant for Staffordshire to director of the North Staffordshire Railway Company. The patronage of these people was crucial to the chapel since the only major and regular source of income apart from this was the rental of pews. In 1856 a number of the free pews reserved for the poor were converted to rented pews. With a Sunday morning congregation of about 600 and an evening congregation of 900, the value of this income was soon appreciated. The grandiose congregation was matched in 1859 with the addition of a classically inspired façade. Ironically, it heralded the decline of the New Connexion in the Potteries. John Ridgway, for years the motivating force behind the movement, died in 1860 and further building programmes at Bethesda and other chapels declined.

The post-Conquest church at Stoke was demolished in 1830 to make way for a new one. Stone from the old church was used to line the bed of a watercourse to Boothen Mill.[25] Later, two semi-circular arches and a pier were re-erected in the churchyard on the site of the old church. The new Commissioners' church of St Peter ad Vincula, designed by Trubshaw and Johnson, built a little to the north of the old site, was started in 1826. The church cost £14,000, but £15,000 was raised by public subscription. It was consecrated in 1830.

Burslem was divided off from the parish of Stoke in 1807. The ancient church of St John the Baptist, of which the west tower still stands, is thought to have been of the 12th or 13th century.[26] The chancel is of 1788 and the remainder of the building dates from slightly earlier in 1717.[27] The Commissioners' gothic inspired church of St Paul's was completed in 1831 at a cost of £10,000 and has since been demolished.

In 1760 John Wesley visited Burslem for the first time, preaching from horseback outside the *Leopard Inn*. He thought of it as a scattered community of potters, an observation that was radically altered by his visit in 1781. The rise of the pottery industry had brought workers from all directions; housing had swallowed up open spaces. Wesley saw this with a mixture of shock and opportunity. The phenomenal growth had created a town in which he believed he could make many a convert.

A chapel had been built in 1766 and by 1787 Burslem was a Methodist stronghold. The Burslem Sunday School was started in that year also and

soon acquired great popularity and support, among the people at large, for its usefulness in instilling, into the rapidly increasing youthful population, the

38 The lower end of Piccadilly in Hanley in about 1912. Albion Street on the right leads to the Town Hall and the wrought iron railings marking the entrance to the underground toilets.

elements of religious and general knowledge, and withdrawing them from vagrant and vicious habits on the Sabbath-day. By the pains bestowed in this School, the seeds of self-culture were sown.[28]

A large library was accumulated by subscription and the classes in reading, writing and recitation, and the accomplishments of the students, were noted by contemporary commentators. This was an interdenominational school, originally proposed by the itinerant Wesleyan preacher Richard Rodda. The school grew beyond all expectations, having 1,700 pupils by 1816 and branches in Longport and Norton. A new chapel was built in 1796 and was enlarged in 1816 to accommodate nearly 1,300 people.

In 1827 it was decided by the Methodist Conference that reading and writing were not subjects that should be taught in Sunday schools. The Burslem school objected so strongly to this that in 1836 the teachers were locked out. Following a public meeting, it was decided to build a new chapel and school at Hilltop. Other Sunday schools continued to teach secular subjects; there was a strong belief that the Sunday schools were the only means of education available to the children of the workers. At a time when children from the age of five or six upwards worked long hours in the factories, the time spent at Sunday school was seen by many children as relief. Others, like the critical and complaining Arnold

39   Piccadilly in the 1970s. The Regent Theatre can be seen clearly on the left.

Bennett, saw it as drudgery and disciplinarian, perhaps a view resulting from the speech impediment which must surely have affected his early education.[29]

The other pottery towns were quick to adopt Methodism in its various forms. We have seen the importance of the New Connexion in Hanley. The first Methodist chapel in that town was only a year old in 1784 when John Wesley visited and claimed it was too small for the congregation. The secession of the New Connexion severely depleted their numbers but by 1819 the Society had recovered sufficiently to build the 770-seat Charles Street Chapel. Wesleyan Methodism remained an influential force in the Potteries. There were 17 Wesleyan chapels in 1851 with congregations numbering

up to 550 at Charles Street in Hanley and 800 at Swan Bank in Burslem.

Primitive Methodism was another potent force in the Potteries, having been established in 1812 at a huge open air meeting at Mow Cop, a folly erected on the border between Staffordshire and Cheshire in 1754. The seeds for the movement had been sown several years earlier by Hugh Bourne and William Clowes. Hugh Bourne converted to Methodism in 1799 and soon had an ardent group of followers as he preached to the 'ungodly' colliers around Harriseahead. Open air preaching and meetings were central to his doctrine and practice and he was inspired by reports from America of huge camps celebrating the word of God. He organised a

40 Mow Cop, birthplace of Primitive Methodism. The castle was built in 1754 as a folly to catch the eye when viewed from Rode Hall and Great Moreton in Cheshire. It stands on an outcrop some 1,000 feet high. Mow Cop is split between Cheshire and Staffordshire but the church of St Thomas, dating from 1842, is in the latter.

meeting at Mow Cop in May 1807, which was dismissed as improper by the June 1807 Methodist Conference. In 1808 Bourne was expelled from the Conference, eventually taking with him his group of followers that included William Clowes. Clowes was a reformed drinker and gambler who converted to Methodism in 1805. He soon became a close friend to Bourne and was himself expelled from the Conference in 1810.

Five

Wealth and Welfare

Between 1833 and 1842 Trentham Hall was rebuilt at a cost of £123,000. It now has the dubious honour of being one of the few demolished buildings given a full description in the works of Pevsner.[1] The architect was Sir Charles Barry and Pevsner claims the building as important as the Houses of Parliament. The 2nd Marquess of Stafford had been elevated to the level of a duke when he married the Duchess of Sutherland, who at the time was one of the wealthiest women in the country. In 1833 their son inherited the estate and immediately began rebuilding the Hall. Barry's design was an asymmetrical and Italianate villa which was to become the model for Osborne House on the Isle of Wight and, subsequently, for many other houses in Britain and in Germany.

The Sutherlands were by no means an aristocratic family living in isolation on their estates. Trentham was one of the earliest stately homes to be opened to the public. During Wakes Week brass bands played in the grounds to entertain the growing crowds of people who visited. Millicent Sutherland-Leveson-Gower (1867–1955) was such a tireless campaigner for the improvement of working conditions in the pottery industry, that many manufacturers considered her to be meddling and called her 'Meddlesome Millie'. She was deeply concerned about the incidence of lead poisoning in the industry and infant mortality rates. Arnold Bennett characterised her as the Countess of

Chell, who lived at Sneyd Hall and was known as 'Interfering Iris' in *The Card*.[2]

> The Countess at this period was busying herself with the policemen of the Five Towns. In her exhaustive passion for philanthropy, bazaars and platforms, she had already dealt with orphans, the aged, the blind, potter's asthma, crèches, churches, chapels, schools, economic cookery, the smoke-nuisance, country holidays, Christmas puddings and blankets, healthy musical entertainment, and barmaids. The excellent and beautiful creature was suffering from a dearth of subjects when the policemen occurred to her.[3]

The Duchess was greatly troubled by her privileged position and its stark contrast with the plight of the poor and the sick. She acted to take children out of the area at least once a year on a holiday in the countryside at Hanchurch. Inspired by the Countess of Warwick, her half-sister, she also threw open the ancestral home at Trentham for the so-called 'cripples treats'. In an article in the *Pall Mall Magazine* in 1904 she described the scene of children suffering from physical and mental disabilities enjoying the peace and beauty of her gardens, and the shock she experienced on seeing just how many children were suffering.

In 1901 the Duchess set up the Potteries and Newcastle Cripples Guild. It aimed to provide children with a 'friend' who would seek access to the best possible medical treatment and to diversionary therapies. Using her influence and social contacts, she established a partnership with Dame Agnes Hunt, who operated an open air hospital in Baschurch in

41 Trentham Hall, home of the Duke and Duchess of Sutherland. The Hall's design by Sir Charles Barry, architect of the Houses of Parliament, set the standard for stately homes in the late 19th century but was unfortunately demolished in 1912. Today the gardens survive and are open to the public although there is speculation about their future.

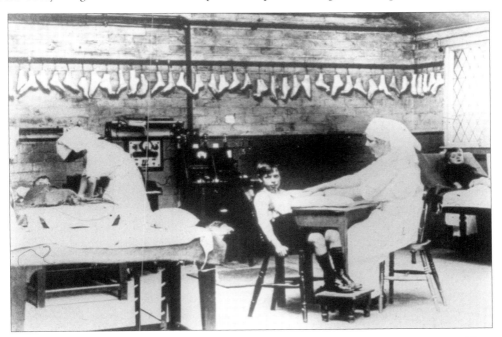

42 A clinic at the Hartshill Orthopaedic Hospital in about 1925. The moulds were used by the cobbler to make corrective footwear. The hospital was in part the realisation of the work of the Duchess of Sutherland.

43 Dame Agnes Hunt and Sir Robert Jones visit work in progress on 16 April 1931. They are seen here with staff from the Hartshill hospital and clinics at Leek, Lichfield, Stafford and Congleton. The extensions to the hospital were dedicated to Rosemary, Viscountess Ednam, daughter of the Duchess of Sutherland.

Shropshire for children from Trentham. Before its move to Hartshill in 1918, the hospital found alternative accommodation at Hanchurch. Hunt's hospital was literally run from farm buildings and had a remarkable success rate in the treatment of childhood disabilities. She persuaded Robert Jones, an eminent surgeon based in Liverpool, to visit Baschurch each month and operate on children and to provide splints and frames. Baschurch became the world's first open air orthopaedic hospital and the model for subsequent national schemes in the 20th century. To raise funds, Millicent held a huge bazaar and fête between 15 and 18 July 1908, with the Princess of Wales acting as patron. The first day was opened by the Crown Princess of Sweden, the second by the

Duchess of Portland, the third by the Countess of Dudley and the final day by His Imperial Highness the Grand Duke Michael of Russia, who was at the time living at Keele Hall. Millicent obviously held back on nothing to achieve her dreams.

The event raised £5,000 and proved to many that the Duchess was more than the shallow caricature of Bennett's writings. The money was used to build the convalescent home at Hanchurch that opened in 1911. Children requiring surgery were sent to Hunt's hospital at Baschurch and spent their convalescence at Hanchurch. Unfortunately Hanchurch was not the ideal location and a clinic under Dr William Mitchell-Smith was set up in Longton, but it was hopelessly inadequate to cope with the

44 The sadly derelict principal entrance and conservatories at Trentham Hall.

45   The Sutherland family's mausoleum at Trentham, the only Grade 1 listed building in the area.

numbers of children brought to it. Within weeks there were over 500 children registered at the clinic.[4] With the former mayor of Burslem, Sydney Malkin, acting as guarantor, £2,000 was raised to purchase the Longfields Estate at Hartshill, former home of pottery manufacturer Herbert Minton, and the hospital was opened on 13 July 1918 by Sir Robert Jones. Sir Joseph Cook laid the foundation stone for the proposed operating theatre on the same occasion. Cook was a former pitworker from Silverdale who had emigrated to Australia and who, at the outbreak of war, had risen to be Prime Minister.

Concern was expressed about the location at Hartshill. It was, after all, in the centre of the industrial belt of the Potteries. Much of

the treatment provided by Hunt, who acted as supervisor at Hartshill for a short while, depended on fresh air. Hartshill was a suburb that attracted many of the wealthy members of society. It was higher in elevation than most of the surrounding district and smoke from the potbanks was blown away and dispersed. The site also came with about ten acres of land in which the patients could convalesce. Within years the hospital claimed to have cured eighty per cent of both in-patients and out-patients. The inadequacies of the buildings were recognised by Lady Ednam, daughter of Millicent, who launched an appeal for funds to extend and develop the hospital in 1929.

Millicent's links with the Potteries weakened when the family decided to move to their

46 Two images of the Audley Hospital Saturday, an annual fundraising event. Both photographs were taken at the turn of the 20th century. In one a stall has been set up outside the church wall, selling buttonholes and nosegays. Girls would also take baskets of buttonholes out amongst the crowds who came to see the procession. The hospitals were dependent on such events for funding. The second image shows the children taking part in the procession. Adults who took part often marched in fancy dress.

47 A view of the Town Hall in Longton before 1900, with what looks like a public speaker drawing a crowd. Elsewhere street traders sell their wares.

estates in Scotland in 1907. Pollution from the Potteries, particularly in the River Trent that flowed through the Trentham estate, had become unbearable. Having been offered to the Borough of Stoke-on-Trent and rejected, Trentham Hall was demolished in 1911. The Sutherland family, despite no longer being attached to Trentham, retained a majority holding in the Trentham Gardens Company set up in 1933. The Duke of Sutherland died

in 1913 and, with the outbreak of war in 1914, the Duchess signed up with the Red Cross, serving in Belgium. After the war she chose to live in France, only returning to Hartshill in 1926. She died in France in 1955.[5] Her daughter Rosemary was briefly to display the glamour and qualities of her mother. She had been proposed to by the Prince of Wales, later the Duke of Windsor. In 1919 she married the Viscount Ednam, a close friend of the Prince.

48 Dispelling the myth that Stoke and the northern Midlands were constantly grey, these gardens in full bloom were the pride of their owners.

Tragically, on 9 December 1929, the same day she announced the creation of a fund to extend the hospital, their son was killed in a traffic accident. In July 1930 Rosemary herself was killed in a flying accident. The fund attracted such public sympathy that the new wing to the hospital was ready for the Prince of Wales to open on 15 November 1931.

If open spaces were seen as important in the rehabilitation of patients suffering from a range of illnesses, then they were also seen as important to the health of the town as a whole. By the 1850s suggestions were being made that public parks be provided by the local authorities. It was John Ridgway who dashed all hopes of the new Borough of Hanley providing the first park,

when he, as first mayor, decided the town had a greater duty to serve the dead than the living. The space earmarked for a public park was created a cemetery. It was Longton that pioneered the first public park.

Annual open days had been a feature of Trentham Park for a number of years. As many as 30,000 people visited the Park on Trentham Thursday in 1850. Such were the numbers of people that the shops closed for the day. People arrived on foot, by train or any other vehicle. They played games, danced to the music of numerous travelling musicians and bands, found their future marriage partner, took a picnic or simply strolled around the gardens. Ridgway's unfavourable view was not an isolated reaction.

49   Queen Mary on the occasion of the opening of the City General Hospital in 1925.

The churches objected to the immorality of the event, along with the Wakes Weeks, and manufacturers baulked at the loss of working time. As church leaders and manufacturers were often one and the same, in addition to being representatives in the town councils, this was strong opposition.

The Duke of Sutherland, however, was nothing if not innovative. The area around Longton was developing: Florence, named after the Duke's daughter, had been laid out in the 1860s with housing to accommodate the growing numbers of miners and their families, Normacot followed in 1875, and Dresden soon

afterwards. In 1879 the Duke declared that a park should be provided to serve this community but his plans were hampered by the lack of an effective Town Council. After 1886 these suburbs formed a part of Longton, and the new mayor, John Aynsley, another manufacturer, began talking to the Duke. In January 1887 the Duke's offer of about forty-five acres was enthusiastically accepted by the Corporation. A public subscription was set up to meet the cost of laying out the park. The Duke gave a sum of money to cover the cost of building a brick wall around the site. Aynsley gave £1,000 of his own money and other

50 The rose garden in Burslem Park. The park was opened in 1893 and made use of former farming and derelict land littered with pit shafts.

manufacturers gave willingly. Collections in factories and other places of work helped raise the outstanding sum. At a special ceremony in March 1887 the mayor cut the first sod and the mayoress planted trees on the site of the first cutting. The workers were given a few hours off in the late afternoon to watch the ceremony, at the end of which bread was distributed amongst the crowd. The park was opened to the public on 25 July 1888 amidst great public celebrations. It had been stocked with plants, trees and shrubs donated by the Sutherlands. The Duke himself commented,

> We all know how necessary lungs are for the human frame. Open spaces are quite as necessary to those who toil much indoors and in a smoky town.[6]

It was a sentiment echoed by Lord Dartmouth when he opened Burslem Park in April 1893. Commenting on the huge social benefits of a park, he referred to their part in the health of the citizens, their role as 'the lungs of the people'.

Despite the hyperbole, the poorer sections of society soon found themselves excluded from many of the facilities offered in the parks. In 1899 it cost the equivalent of a half-day's pay to go boating for an hour. Skating had been allowed on the frozen lake since 1890 but the cost by the turn of the century was 3d. for children and 6d. for adults. In Longton Park it cost 2s. 6d. a day for a fishing permit. In 1907 the North Staffordshire Miners Federation had to find £100 for a permit to hold a rally in the park and to pay for any damage.[7]

51   Queen's Park in Longton. The park was the first to be opened in the Potteries and made use of land given by the Duke of Sutherland. It was opened with great ceremony in July 1888.

Following a large public meeting in 1890, the mayor of Hanley pursued the acquisition of land for a public park. Hidden amidst the rhetoric of the benefits to the health of the people was the cost of a halfpenny a week to the working population of the town. The Cauldon Grounds was the first section of the 100-acre site to be completed and was opened by Alderman E.J. Hammersley in July 1894. Between that date and the opening of the rest of the park on Jubilee Day 1897, many hopes were expressed about the improvement of the physical appearance of the town as well as the improved health and morals of the citizens.

The other towns followed suit. Burslem Park, designed by Thomas Mawson, who also designed Hanley Park, and including ladies' and gentlemen's reading rooms, was opened in 1893. Etruria Park opened in 1904 and those at Northwood and Tunstall in 1907 and 1908. Fenton Park came much later. Construction began in 1918 using German war prisoners but the park was not opened until 1924. Stoke did not lay out a park.

The Potteries celebrated three Wakes. Originally of religious intent, the Wakes celebrations had become a time of amusement and feasting, to a hedonistic extent according to some contemporary reporters, and represented an escape from the drudgery of everyday life and work. The extent of the 'hedonism' is in part explained by the lack of facilities provided by the various local authorities and manufacturers. In other industrial cities the owners of wealth had taken pride in the infrastructure and indulged in competition with other cities,

52 Stoke station. Along the platform, below the clock, a truck is stacked with milk churns. A young boy, possibly an apprentice, accompanies the porter just beyond the foreground trucks, one of which clearly displays the Staffordshire Knot emblem of the North Staffordshire Railway Company.

whereas the Potteries limited themselves to internal competition. This was to have repercussions in the 20th century when the region had to face the issue of the post-industrial economy. The Wakes totally disrupted normal routine activities and were seen by many outside the area as the only means of mass entertainment. The pottery industry was organised on a small scale, often in family-run factories, and a managerial grouping was largely absent. The Wakes compounded the issue of social regulation that had its roots in the structure of the core industry.

Burslem Wakes were held during the week following the Nativity of St John the Baptist on 24 June. Tunstall Wakes were held in late July to celebrate St Margaret, the patron saint of Wolstanton parish church, and the Stoke Wakes focused on the first Sunday in August. Church leaders as well as manufacturers were again amongst the principal opponents of the Wakes. Josiah Wedgwood himself complained bitterly about time lost to the celebrations. They complained about the amusements, too, suggesting they were excessive, immoral and licentious. The manufacturers, already establishing a regime

53 The *North Stafford Hotel* was opened in 1849 by the North Staffordshire Railway Company. It forms one side of Winton Square, one of the county's finest examples of Victorian planning. The square featured a statue of Josiah Wedgwood from 1863.

of strict control over their workforces, wished to extend this control to cover every aspect of their lives. The authorities, already controlling social relationships through the systems of relief and the workhouses, sought to introduce more regulation into the lives of the people. Bull baiting remained popular until 1835 when the 'sport' was made illegal. The game of prison-bars was often played out between teams from the different towns or from places of work. It involved members of teams being taken prisoner by the opposition until they were rescued by their colleagues. It was a boisterous game played out on open ground. Other sports and amusements included boxing rings, music, acrobatics, horse racing and gambling. The Temperance groups, Sunday schools, church leaders and manufacturers organised alternative galas, tea parties, picnics and trips to the countryside in an attempt to bring the Wakes celebrations to an end. Ultimately it was the increasingly centralised and commercial aspects of the wakes, requiring regulation, that curtailed the activities.

As bureaucracy established itself the Wakes were transformed into the Potters Holidays. The Tunstall Board of Health banned various sideshows in 1876 and processions and athletics

54 To entice people to use the railways, the North Staffordshire Railway Company issued several series of postcards illustrating some of the locations to which their trains ran. Rudyard Lake was one of the most popular destinations with day-trippers from the Potteries.

galas were organised. In 1879 the Burslem Board of Health, which was made up of pottery manufacturers, successfully banned the Wakes, but the disappointed revellers won a referendum reinstating the celebrations the following year and were supported by the local clergy. They argued that it was only a minority who abused the event with drunkenness and that the levels of absenteeism resulting from over drinking was not noticeably higher after the Wakes than during more normal times. However, soon after it was accepted that a single Wakes Week would be observed in the Potteries and the timing of the Stoke Wakes became the focus. The celebrations were held in Hanley and by 1911 roundabouts, organs, bazaars, sideshows of various kinds, acrobatics, performing fleas and the like covered an area between Market Square and Crown Bank and the adjacent

streets. Only after 1923 was the event moved to an area of land off Regent Road. It remained a popular time in the annual calendar. Many people counted the Wakes as part of their holiday.

The idea of going away on holiday was not easily entertained until the advent of the railways in 1830, when the Manchester to Liverpool line was opened. The success was immediate and lines soon linked these cities with Birmingham and London. Almost over-night roads lost passengers to the much faster and cheaper railway. Towns and villages that embraced the railways, or were ideally situated to accept a station, faced rapid growth whilst those by-passed by the system became back-waters.

The North Staffordshire Railway Company monopolised development of the railways

55 Refreshment facilities were provided by the North Staffordshire Railway Company at Rudyard Lake.

56 Bagnall Cross on a postcard from about 1900. The comment written on the reverse discusses the existence of beauty spots in the area.

57 The Manifold Valley was another popular destination. This idyllic scene of Wetton Bridge contrasts so markedly with the streets of Stoke.

around the Potteries. The main line between Longport, Etruria, Stoke and Stone became the backbone of a system of branch lines that extended to Leek in the east and Market Drayton in the west. Work began in 1847 on Stoke station, which was completed by 1848. The railway company based its headquarters in the boardroom above the station and owned the prestigious *North Staffordshire Hotel* opposite, one of a series of hotels built and operated by the company. The system of lines connecting all the towns in a loop with the main line became known affectionately as the 'Loopline'.

The company sought to take over freight haulage but faced stiff competition from the canal system. Under the Railways Acts of 1846 and 1847, railway companies were empowered to buy out the canal companies, a merger the

Trent and Mersey Canal Company actively sought to reduce losses. The North Staffordshire Railway Company at first maintained the canals as feeders to the railway network. With stone quarrying and mineral extraction away from the new railways, it was particularly important to maintain a means of transporting heavy raw products, and the canals had been cut specifically for this purpose. They provided a much-needed source of income for the company. As the effects of the railways began to bite, however, mining and quarrying companies sought to reduce their transportation costs by using the railways and slowly the canals entered into decline.[8]

The railways were to be used extensively by Potters moving around the region and going further afield on holiday. In 1850 about 20,000

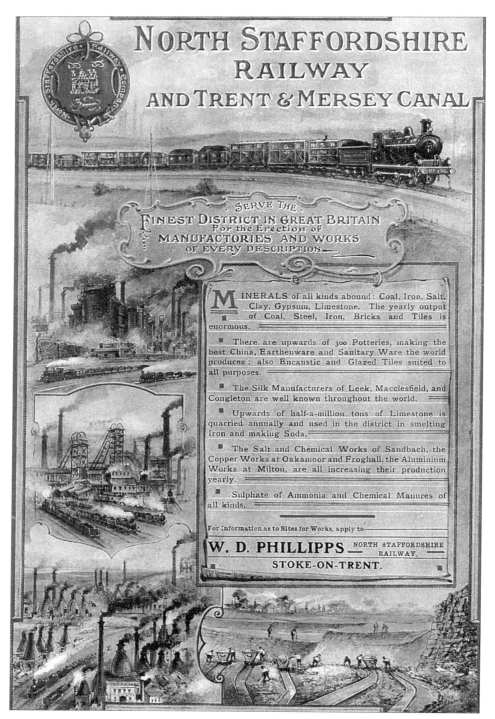

58 A poster advertising the North Staffordshire Railway. It illustrates the company's service to industries ranging from the limestone quarries to the 300 or so potbanks and the steelworks.

people went on excursions during the Stoke Wakes. Their destinations varied but included Chester, Liverpool, Rudyard Lake and the Churnet Valley. Rudyard Lake had been created in 1797 to feed the Trent and Mersey and Caldon canal systems and the grant of shooting and fishing rights opened the reservoir to those living beside the lake. A railway to the lake built in the 1840s brought the area within easy reach of the people of Stoke and it soon proved a popular destination for day trips. After 1850 the North Staffordshire Railway Company operated tearooms at Rudyard and after 1851 it was involved in legal disputes over an annual fête and regatta on the lake. Local residents, organised by Fanny Bostock, were bitterly opposed to the suggestion. The first regatta organised by the company, at Easter 1851, attracted about 10,000 visitors. The fears of the residents were realised, with litter and damage to property, not to mention the flaunting of fishing and shooting rights. The five years long court battle fought against the railway company resulted in a ruling forbidding leisure activities on the lake. Despite this, about 4,000 attended the crossing by Blondin on a tightrope some 100 feet above its surface in 1864, by which time regattas and one off events were becoming the norm rather than the fiercely opposed exception. Only after 1904 was the railway company allowed to realise the full commercial potential of the lake and a station there opened in 1905.

It was at Rudyard that John Lockwood Kipling met his future wife Alice Macdonald in 1863. They were married two years later before he took up a post as head of a school of art in Bombay. On 30 December 1865 Joseph Rudyard Kipling was born, later the winner of the Nobel Prize for Literature. He was named after his grandfather and the spot at which his parents had met.[9]

During the Wakes trips were organised for every day of the week. In 1878 about 40,000 left the Potteries for North Wales, the Isle of Man, Buxton, Matlock and Southport.[10] These more exotic destinations were still beyond the means of the ordinary workers. Many used the railways to visit Rudyard, Alton Towers or Trentham Park. From 1848 there had been a station at Trentham principally serving the Duke of Sutherland's mineral interests. During the 1850s, with further developments at the Hall, the Duke had his architect design a new station in keeping with his residence. The main purpose of the station was to accommodate the huge retinue of people, goods, carriages and livestock the Duke would take with him on his twice yearly trip to his estates at Dunrobin in Scotland, or the retinues of his distinguished guests at Trentham. One such visitor was the Shah of Persia, who arrived in June 1873. The Prince of Wales visited in 1880.[11] A later branch station served the park and was the means by which most day-trippers reached their destination. The numbers of visitors increased with the building of the ballroom in 1931 and a fine art deco swimming pool in 1935.

Six

The Modern Era

By the turn of the 20th century the movement for federation, bringing the six towns under one local authority, was gaining momentum. In 1895 it had gained the support of the Duke of Sutherland, a further attempt at federation failed in 1901, the existing towns still possessing interests they would not relinquish. Federation was not achieved until 1910 when the County Borough of Stoke-on-Trent was created. The new borough covered some 11,139 acres and had a population of 234,000. Its first mayor was Cecil Wedgwood, who later died on active service in 1916. In 1925 the County Borough

was raised to the status of City and the title of Lord Mayor was conferred on 10 July 1928. The first to hold the position was Thomas Clarke Wild. The position of Lord Mayor was to remain largely unchanged until 2002, when the City elected its first Mayor, Mike Wolfe.

Life for the citizens of the new County Borough changed little. Housing remained poor in quality. On first impression some housing appeared spacious. Elizabeth Fanshawe described the three-bedroomed house with three downstairs rooms she grew up in at Penkhull in the 1920s,[1] but lacked indoor

59 The old Town Hall in Hanley. This building also housed the police force and was opened in 1845. It was taken over by Lloyd's Bank in 1886 but has since been demolished. The town hall was relocated to the *Queen's Hotel*, a building with French influences, in 1888.

60 The Sutherlands of Trentham built the Sutherland Institute in Longton between 1897 and 1899 to commemorate the Queen's Diamond Jubilee. The frieze depicts the pottery industry and dates from 1909.

61 The Clock Tower in Tower Square, Tunstall dates from 1893 and marks the site of the original town hall. Pevsner described the Town Hall of 1885 behind as 'a sort of Italian, ill-defined'. It cost £14,000 and the lower floor was leased out as retail units and to the National Provincial Bank at one time.

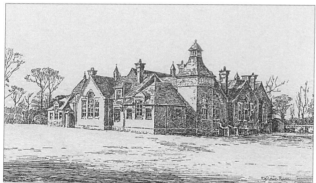

62 (above) Burslem Town Hall seen from the corner of St John's Square. The angel on top of the tower is a well-known landmark.

63 (left) Penkhull Council School in an illustration that shows clearly how separate Penkhull remained from the rest of the Potteries.

facilities. There were many instances of groups of ten houses sharing a solitary tap and lavatory. Cooking centred around the range in the kitchen which served as the living room too. During the 1920s lighting downstairs was provided by gas mantles; upstairs her family used candles. At Penkhull a group of houses known as The Square had been built in about 1802 by Josiah Spode. Each house consisted of a living room, a small scullery and two bed-rooms above. They were extended in 1907 and two rows of communal toilets were built. The description is not that different from that of the houses built by Wedgwood at Etruria. Elizabeth Stringer, who was born in 1904, recalled that after the death of her father in

1906 her family moved from one house to another, not having any food except that given in hand-outs, and no new clothes. On one occasion they were given accommodation in Cobridge but had to move out after spending only one night on the floor of the toilet because everywhere was infested with vermin.[2] In contrast, Eveline Shaw who was born in 1919 grew up in a relatively comfortable house with a large garden. The house was comfortably furnished but still lacked indoor facilities apart from a cold water tap in the kitchen. In the garden her family grew vegetables, a valuable supplement to their diet.[2]

Housing had developed piecemeal and by various small enterprises, resulting in quality and styles differing from street to street and sometimes within streets. The streets formed communities, often very insular in character. There was little movement around the city as workplaces tended to be close by. It has to be said that some of the housing that dates from the late Victorian period was not of too bad a quality. But these were the exceptions. J.B. Priestley described the condition of Potteries housing in the 1930s as 'Victorian industrialism in its dirtiest and most cynical aspect'.[3] By the mid-20th century there was a marked reluctance to move. People preferred not to have to travel to work by bus or by train (or tram up until their demise in the 1920s) and many could not afford to do so. Only the wealthy had started to move to leafy suburbs like Hartshill, Basford, Trentham and the Westlands and, as in most other cities, their larger houses were converted to flats to accommodate more families. The building of high-rise flats was not an option since years of undermining had made the topography too unstable to support such structures. Even today the only building of any significant height is Unity House, a former office block used by

the City and by Staffordshire County Council until its closure in the 1990s.

It was only during the interwar period that the corporation began a programme of house building. There had been an almost complete cessation in house building during the war that led to an acute shortage nationally after 1918. In 1919 the Stoke-on-Trent Council set up its first Housing Committee and under the terms of the Addison Housing Act of the same year set about redressing the problem within its boundaries. Between 1921 and 1939 over 8,000 council houses were built around the city.[4] Estates such as Bentilee, Abbey Hulton, Carmountside, High Lane and the houses erected along Trent Vale by the Sutton Housing Trust enjoyed a density ranging between 4 and 14 houses per acre, as opposed to the 40 to 50 norm of the later Victorian period. Even so, the sheer size of estates such as Bentilee poses social problems for the City Council in the form of welfare and education provision.

Atmospheric pollution from heavy industry was a cause for concern. The photographs of William Blake record the magnitude of the problem and the memories of those who were children during the first half of the 20th century emphasise it. Angela Mellor, who was born in 1915, recalls that although her family home had a garden little would grow in it, and because of the pollution around Shelton where they lived, autumn seemed to come early, with leaves falling off their tree from about June. Graham Davies, who was born in 1930, recalls the streets being blacked out by the down draught from the potbank chimneys.[5] Up to the Clean Air Acts of the 1950s the air around Stoke remained filthy. The potbanks, Shelton bar, the Michelin, the railways and countless home fires contributed to the problem. Years of pollution took their toll on the population.

64 This series of photographs illustrated the problems of airborne pollution in the Potteries. Individual images carried ironic titles like 'Stoke-on-Trent. Always Merry and Bright'. Or 'Fresh Air from the Potteries'.

Until only recently diseases causing the most fatalities in the Potteries were those related to the lungs. The local hospitals had open air wards for tuberculosis sufferers.

The North Staffordshire Royal Infirmary is perhaps the oldest of the hospitals in the city. It began as a House of Recovery at Etruria in 1802 but this location soon became unsuitable and the newly named Infirmary moved to a site between Cobridge and Etruria in 1819. Here it remained until 1869 when it transferred

to a new site at Hartshill, already noted as a clean suburb that suffered little from atmospheric pollution. The foundation stone was laid by the Prince of Wales in 1866 and the new hospital buildings cost about £32,000. It was during the visit of George V and Queen Mary in 1925 that the name of 'Royal Infirmary' was adopted. On the same visit City status was awarded to Stoke-on-Trent. At a bazaar held to help raise money the young Oliver Lodge demonstrated the new marvel of the age, electricity! The history of hospitals in the Potteries is one of public donations and of workers subscribing from their wages. This was an insurance scheme that helped cover the cost of treatment when the subscriber fell ill. It also made the hospital very much a part of the community as a whole. People felt that they had a stake in it and this was a significant loss with the introduction of the National Health Service in 1948. The City General Hospital was established around the workhouse buildings on London Road.

A cottage hospital was set up in Longton in 1870. It treated 106 patients per year and a further 252 outpatients on a budget of £1,175.[6] It was forced to move after 1887 because of encroachment by local industry, just like the

65 The North Staffordshire Infirmary seen from Queen's Road and the cemetery. The Prince of Wales laid the foundation stone for this building in 1866.

66 Saggar makers at work in a potbank. Saggars were vessels into which wares were placed in the kiln to protect them.

67   Paint work in 1905 was almost exclusively women's work.

House of Recovery at Etruria nearly seventy years earlier. The Duke of Sutherland again generously donated land at the new site in Normacot. Two brothers set up the Haywood Hospital between Burslem and Tunstall. Their bequest allowed for a cottage hospital and dispensary and for the support of convalescing patients while at the seaside or an inland spa. After the First World War the hospital was rebuilt and became known as the Burslem Haywood and Tunstall War Memorial Hospital, 'The Haywood'.

Potters tried to work for the same company as long as they could, often for the same firm as their forebears. There developed a deep sense of loyalty which it was hoped would see the individual through hard times. This loyalty was formalised when apprentices swore not to take a job in another potbank for the duration of their seven-year apprenticeship. As many potters did piecework, proof of their skills, speed and loyalty was important.

Potbanks lacked social amenities. Unlike the other large employers, such as Michelin and Shelton Bar, potbanks did not have a social club and many lacked a room in which employees could stop for a break. Being on piecework, the potters were indisposed to take a break in any case, eating their sandwiches at their workbench. The workplace was a finely tuned social institution by the 1950s. It reflected many of the divisions and prejudices that had developed. Certain tasks were exclusively male, such as throwing the clay. After this part of the process became mechanised it remained a masculine stronghold, and output became a matter of male pride. Fully automated systems were capable of making 20 cups a minute whereas an experienced maker who used moulds could produce about three. The maker was paid according to the output of his team and passed the wages on. The team would include a mouldrunner, a handler (who attached the handles), and the sponger, who ensured a smooth finish to the cup. An experienced woman who sliced the clay for the handles used a large blade for the process and could slice 900 handles a day. This was monotonous work with little opportunity for a break. Wages were also weighted in favour of the men. A maker could earn about £8 17s. per week before overtime. A male cleaner earned £8, the same as the top rates paid to skilled women workers. Engravers, the elite of the potbank workers, earned between £11 and £13 per week. The Ministry of Labour had suggested that the average weekly wage for skilled workers in the manufacturing industries was £14 per week. After the Second World War there was an increase in the number of immigrants to the city, particularly from Eastern Europe. The Polish community was perhaps the largest such group and they rarely achieved the higher status tasks within the potbank.

The pottery decorators were also on piecework, and this group of workers tended to be women. They were paid only for their output and the time spent mixing their paints was unpaid. Good paintresses were paid about 6d. per plate and produced a decorated plate every five minutes. Large runs of a particular decoration suited these women; as they became more familiar with it, their productivity increased, as did their wages. New decorations and, worse still, frequent changes of decoration, invariably meant time lost learning the new style and a reduction in wages. On occasion particularly when the potbank was trying to complete an order to time, skilled workers would be taken from their usual work to cover another part of the process: paintresses would be moved to silk-screening; silk-screeners would be moved to the warehouse, and so on. This too meant a reduction in wages as the workers who were moved were taken off their piecework rate and put on a general rate of about 1s. 11d. an hour. When they were normally earning about £5 to £8 per week this was a huge reduction for the women.

The unions were not a strong force in the pottery industry. By 1960 the union had negotiated a guaranteed working week of 32 hours for everybody, reduced from 44 hours, paid holidays and a five-day working week. There was a non-strike practice observed by the workers, although a strike could not have been effective unless it involved the whole industry. This was more or less impossible because the industry was made up of numerous small businesses whose workforces had developed their sense of loyalty and attachment. Neither was there an infrastructure to organise a strike: there were no shop stewards in the workplace.

But by the 1950s the city was suffering a recession. It was not uncommon to walk streets of boarded-up houses and fish and chip shops and closed down public houses. Smaller pottery manufacturing companies were closing down and as they did so the buildings were demolished. For various reasons they were rarely built upon and by 1960 about ten per cent of the city was officially derelict land. A Reconstruction Plan was drafted in 1951 that urged industry to relocate to the outskirts of the urban area, but this was never a realistic option. The population of the country as a whole was by this time predominantly urban

68   The sheer size of some bottle ovens can be seen clearly in this view of Ridgway's Bedford Works at Shelton in 1958.

and in Stoke there were about 12,000 people on the waiting list for a house by 1953. During the 1950s and 1960s over 21,000 people left the Potteries in search of work and better housing.[7]

The pottery industry has not been the only industry to suffer in north Staffordshire. Of the three core industries in the region it is the only survivor, steel and coal having now vanished from the city.

The iron and steel works first appeared on a large scale some 300 years ago. Blast furnaces first appeared in Staffordshire at Cannock Wood near Hednesford. Furnaces at Apedale, Biddulph, Fenton Park and at Silverdale quickly followed them. Their efficiency was restricted by the use

69   Norton Colliery in about 1895.

of wood and charcoal as fuel and they were superseded by coal-fired furnaces as developed by Abraham Darby in Shropshire. In the 1780s the introduction of coke allowed superior quality iron to be produced. Granville's site at Etruria was above rich seams of coal and included some of the deepest pits in the region, such as the Racecourse Pit (actually dug beneath a horse-racing course that closed in 1840) and Hanley Deep Pit, that had a shaft some 1,500 feet deep. By 1839 work had begun at Shelton on the three blast furnaces that produced their first iron in 1841. These furnaces were on a strip of land between Cobridge Road and Mill Street (later Etruria Road). They were the brainchild of the 1st Earl Granville, Marquis of Stafford, who

leased the land from the Duchy of Lancaster, an institution that held many of the mineral rights in the Potteries. It neighboured the Etruria works of Josiah Wedgwood and had access to the Trent and Mersey Canal. A fourth blast furnace was added to this trio several years later and an extra four brought the total number of blast furnaces on the site to eight.

The earl died in 1846 and his son, the 2nd Earl, took over the family business. He maintained control of the blast furnaces but created a partnership to run the newly formed Shelton Bar Iron Company in 1851. The company went from strength to strength, even winning a Silver Medal at the 1855 Paris Exhibition. This was followed with a Bronze Medal at

70 The opening of the Minnie Pit in 1872. The pit was to be the scene of one of the major colliery disasters in the North Staffordshire field when, in 1918, 155 miners lost their lives.

71   The Chatterley Whitfield Rescue Team in about 1905. Rescue teams within an 11-mile radius of a colliery were compulsory after 1911.

London in 1862, a Gold Medal at Paris in 1878 and a further Gold at Melbourne in 1880. On 10 July 1866 the Shelton Iron and Steel Company was created. By 1888 Shelton Bar was in full production and over 3,000 people were employed on the site. Granville retained personal ownership of the blast furnaces in addition to his major shareholding in the new company and this remained the situation until after the earl's death in 1891. His son took over and immediately set about amalgamating

all the interests on the site into one company, the Shelton Iron Steel and Coal Company. The company was also responsible for setting up the Hanley Economic Building Society.

It decided to invest in steel as the future of the company and the two furnaces that produced 143 tons of steel a week in 1892 were supplemented with six more by 1905. A 30-inch rolling mill was built powered by a huge steam engine, and a railway network connected further mills and furnaces on the

72   The Winstanley headgear at Chatterley Whitfield.

various parts of the site. In order to improve the quality of the steel, coal was replaced by coke and a Coking Company was established. Coal was brought in from the South Wales fields and the company began to buy out collieries. Florence, Silverdale, Talke and Holditch were all owned by Shelton.

In the interwar years the company was faced with growing wages bills and accumulating debts. In 1920 there was a successful takeover bid by John Summers and Sons Ltd, a firm of steelmakers from Flintshire. As the new owners introduced more mechanisation and output quotas the wrought iron business was closed down. In 1924 the Prince of Wales visited the site to open the new No. 4 coke ovens.

After the war the business lost control of its collieries as the Labour government nationalised the coal mining industry. Between 1951 and 1953 the steel industry was nationalised and the constant swapping between private and public ownership undoubtedly contributed to its post-war decline. The Summers family, to whom ownership reverted in 1953, became reluctant to invest as heavily in the development of Shelton and during the ensuing decade the plant became increasingly out of date. But years of under-investment were reversed when the company decided to spend nearly £19 million on The Grange plant a little to the north of the site and installed Swedish Kaldo converters. They also decided to cast their steel continually rather than pour it into moulds and transport

73   Coal picking on the waste tips at Florence Colliery during the strike of 1912.

it away from the furnaces. In June 1964 the rolling mill opened, superseding the 30-inch mill that had opened in the 1890s.

The plant was again nationalised in 1967 and the following year saw the closure of the coking plant. In 1971 the 18-inch mill was closed down. The British Steel Company switched to supporting plants with access to deep-water wharves in order to import huge quantities of foreign raw materials. Shelton was being used for experimental techniques, which averted complete closure, but the works finally closed in 1978. The rolling mill continued to produce 400,000 tons per year, but this too

ceased production when the last bar was rolled in April 2000.

The demise of the coal industry in north Staffordshire has been a tragic process. Proper exploitation of the region's mineral wealth only started with the coming of the canals and, later, the railways. The development also depended to some extent on the interest of local landholders. In the 1830s the income derived from mineral extraction by the Sneyd estate amounted to a mere one per cent of the total. By 1850 this proportion had risen to thirty-five per cent and by the 1860s to over sixty per cent.[8] But Ralph Sneyd was not particularly

74 Heavy artillery and tanks were used nationally to keep enthusiasm for the First World War effort high. The tank was the latest military development and the presence of one in Stoke-on-Trent attracted large crowds.

75 Young boys, probably trainee miners, coming off shift just before the outbreak of war in 1939. Around their belts they wear lamps and snappin' tins, food boxes designed to keep out rats and other vermin.

76 A newsagent's shop at the corner of Etruria Vale and Etruria Road.

interested in mining, despite the £29,000 it earned him in 1871. Instead he leased his land to those who were.

Earl Granville, on the other hand, doggedly held on to ownership of his blast furnaces at Shelton up until his death in the 1890s. His company became the largest single employer in the area and also the largest single ratepayer. The success of the company must in large part be accredited to the earl, whose personal interest and involvement was a driving force. The Sutherlands at Trentham Hall were also very much involved in the development of industry on their estates. The Florence Colliery was named after the duke's daughter. The duke also established the Stafford Colliery and Iron Works at Great Fenton.

Up until the 1870s there was tremendous growth in the iron and steel and the coal industries. In 1875 coal production was up thirteen per cent on the 1870 figures.[9] By 1880, however, the story was very different. Iron and steel went into recession and many of the larger coal companies that served the industry felt the pinch. The smaller businesses that tended to serve the pottery industry weathered the storm rather better. At the same time the number of smaller mining companies declined as ironmasters like Granville began to buy up the collieries.

In 1872 the North Staffordshire Institute of Mining and Mechanical Engineers was formed specifically to improve mining processes in north Staffordshire. Until then, developments in the local industry trailed behind those in other coalfields. In 1856 it was estimated at just over one million tons per year and by 1870 it was four million. The new colliery masters, from the iron and steel companies, closed inefficient and less productive pits, investing more in deep level extraction. The Hanley Deep Pit had reached 2,650 feet by the early 20th century. By 1900 overall output was exceeding five million tons.

It was this period of mining that created the huge spoil heaps that characterised the landscape. The cost of cleaning the slack from the coal was huge; in some collieries the amount of slack accounted for as much as seventy-five per cent of the extracted material. The heaps intrigued the children of later generations who played amongst them. They were known locally as rucks. One village, that of Old White Hill, which no longer survives, was surrounded by rucks created by waste from the Birchenwood Colliery and Coking Plant and within living memory could only be reached by one very muddy farm track. The pottery industry created its own waste, too, which accumulated in huge hills known as shard rucks.[10]

Seven

The Post-Modern Era

On 14 December 1940 a lone German bomber attacked Stoke-on-Trent. Such raids, targeting industrial sites or military complexes were not uncommon. The Luftwaffe had prioritised targets around the country, some meant for intensive raids, others to be picked at by 'hit and run' aircraft. The raid, possibly by a Junkers JU88, hit Chesterton but fortunately missed the Alexandra Picture House at which a children's matinee had just finished. However, 14 people were killed including three members of the Salvation Army when their hall suffered a direct hit. Another victim was a young girl from London who had been evacuated to Chesterton. During December 1940, 3,793 civilians were killed and 5,244 injured as a result of enemy air raids across the country.

On another occasion the newly built nurses home at the North Staffordshire Royal Infirmary, that had only opened on 27 July 1940 to house 100 nurses, suffered damage before anybody had taken up residence there. The attack disrupted access to several clinics. On one occasion the churchyard at Etruria was hit by a bomb that disturbed a number of graves.[1] On 15 January 1941 bombs damaged houses on Stoke Old Road in Basford. Two were dropped, the second killing eight people who had come out to watch the rescue attempts. A special constable was amongst those killed. Described as a raid on 'a working class district in a Midlands town', several bombs

killed four civilians at Pittshill, and on 1 June 1941 one person was killed when a roof collapsed following a raid on May Bank. Most of these raids affected civilian buildings. The top priority targets of the steelworks, the railways and the sewage plants, with the exception of the hospital, were largely unaffected. There was a standing joke that the planes returning from raids over Manchester and Liverpool missed Stoke because they assumed the city had already been hit. It was a story given some credence when American soldiers passing through Longton on the train exclaimed about the bomb damage.[2]

Other raids caused minor disruption with incendiary devices setting off fires that were easily contained by the firefighting services. A firewatch was set up in Hanley during 1940 but the men received little training. The county as a whole, however, had had plenty of time to prepare for war. From about 1938 Auxiliary Fire Services had been established in both urban and rural communities and equipment had been obtained or requisitioned for the outbreak of war in 1939. Auxiliary firefighters from Stoke attended the fires at Coventry after the city was devastated by air raids between 14 and 15 November 1940. In June 1941 Hartshill suffered

a positive shower of incendiary bombs in and around the Richmond Street allotments. The then vicar of St Andrews was there with us, and he picked up what he thought was a sandbag and plonked it on a smouldering bomb. It was, in fact,

77 Evacuees arrive in the Potteries in about 1939. The girl in the foreground crouches behind a sack with the name Nottingham on it whilst an armband on the right of the photograph carries the abbreviation MCR for Manchester.

a bag of manure, and he almost gassed the whole population of Richmond Street and Penkhull – and the Firewatchers never let him forget it.[3]

By early September 1939 about 30,000 children had been evacuated to Stoke from London and the south east and Manchester.[4] Local families were required to take these children in. Some families were only too pleased to do so since each child billeted with

a family brought an allowance from the government. But these were not the only people to move into the area during the course of the year. By the time of the build up for Operation Overlord the north Staffordshire area had become, in the words of one of its citizens, a 'cosmopolitan' region. French soldiers had arrived in 1940 after the fall of France and were stationed at Trentham where, on

78   The North Staffordshire Home Guard.

25 August, they were visited by King George VI and General de Gaulle. But the city also hosted Greeks and Poles as well as the Americans after their entry into the war. There is at least one account of black Americans being billeted at Leek whilst white Americans were located in Stoke.[5] The GIs were a magnet to local women and were banned from going into Uttoxeter town centre on certain nights of the week. So the women went to the young

soldiers, who waited on a fence just outside the town. Some groups of young people organised bus trips to the Saturday night dances held at the American bases. Warrington and Stone were both popular destinations. There was plenty of food, cigarettes, drink and the ubiquitous stockings. Stone had the added attraction of being the post of Clark Gable, the Hollywood legend, for a short while. He attended the dances where a few moments on

79   Meir Aerodrome on the outskirts of the city saw action as a maintenance and building plant during the war.

the dance floor turned into a lifelong memory for many young Stoke women.

As the men went away to fight, the women of Stoke took up the employment opportunities presented to them. The clearing bank was relocated from Post Office Court in London to the ballroom at Trentham, and although over 900 personnel came with it, local women were also employed. Essential services were maintained by the direct input of women. The police, ambulance and firefighting services all benefited from their dedication. Others found demand for their skills in industry, particularly engineering, and in public transport or the Land

Army. The latter was less popular for it meant working away from home. The munitions factories at Swynnerton and at Radway Green were dependent on the female workforce, which experienced long shifts in highly dangerous working conditions. Accidents were common but the longer term effects of working in the powder rooms, which temporarily stained the women's skin yellow, were not known.

The pottery industry was kept in full production, thereby adding pollution to the miseries of rationing and the air raids. The products were shipped overseas, principally to America, earning the country valuable foreign

80 Lamb Street in Hanley. The large building on the left with the sunblind next door to Barclay's Bank is Huntbach's.

81 Piccadilly in Hanley in about 1948. In the centre of the photograph is the Chimes Building, the original location of the Hanley branch of Boots the Chemists.

82 These ladies are at the Floral Hall in Tunstall for a dinner dance in 1952.

83 The interior of St Andrew's Church, Honeywall.

currency and investment. The people were still described as proud but obviously poor; dressed, in one contemporary account, in dark and shabby clothing. The city has a long and proud connection with the Staffordshire Regiment and the people were used to seeing soldiers walking the streets whilst on leave, and RAF personnel from the base at Meir. They were less used to seeing naval officers and auxiliaries from the HMS *Excalibur* base at Alsager. The blackout was rigorously enforced. Buses still ran, but at night time the cabin was dark and the passengers, having waited in the inevitably long queue, could only find a seat if somebody called out to them.

The standard of living continued to be low after the war. Many families had lost their breadwinners, and on their return the men were placed back in their old jobs. The women who had worked so hard during the war lost

84 Arthur Scargill with members of the North Staffordshire Miners' Wives Action Group. The NSMWAG provided crucial support to distressed mining families during the 1984-5 strike. On the tenth anniversary of the dispute they commissioned the Coal Sculpture that stands in The Potteries Museum & Art Gallery.

their independence again and with it their income. Children were expected to work as soon as they could leave school; there were few opportunities for further education. At about the age of 14, boys could expect to be

85 The impact of large-scale excavation of clay at Trent Vale.

86 Cauldon Low quarry. Limestone extraction has had a devastating impact on the environment.

doing low skilled and menial work such as mixing on the brick press, running as an errand boy, or delivery and collection work; there was shop work for the girls. Apprenticeships were offered in the pottery industry as well as in engineering, particularly with the bus company or at Stoke Works, the construction and maintenance depot for the railway company. In the build up to the Festival of Britain in 1951 there must have seemed little to shout about in cities like Stoke-on-Trent, but the pottery manufacturers played a major role in the celebrations in London. Between the end of the war and 1951 the wares were plain, except those going for export. Britain was re-developing its foreign markets after the

87 This marl hole, dug to extract clay, illustrates the impact of industry on the local environment. Note also the close vicinity of both housing and industrial buildings. The pit is being used as a waste tip.

88 Hanley Park and a quiet day's bowling. This image speaks volumes about the social and environmental benefits of the City's parks.

89 Piccadilly in Hanley, just below the junction with Pall Mall. Further up lies Cheapside. This part of town was often referred to as Little London.

war and the Festival became a showcase for the best being produced at that time, but it was not representative of the day-to-day experience of the man or woman in the street.

By the 1950s and 1960s there was a desperate need for urban renewal in the city as many of the small potbanks and factories closed down and were demolished and the land left derelict. By the end of the 1950s over ten per cent of the city's land was officially derelict. One commentator in 1961 noted that it was difficult to go anywhere in the City without seeing boarded up houses.[6] The Reconstruction Plan of 1951 had argued for the relocation of industry to the outskirts, but in an area where people traditionally lived and worked almost on the same street, this was not realistic. It was a situation comparable with that in the Lancashire cotton towns: when the local industry collapsed the social repercussions were immense.

But the people of Stoke still resented the view that their city was over-polluted, old-fashioned and ugly and a place in which change only happened slowly,[7] a view put forward by a BBC television programme in 1960. Their arguments focused not only on the amenities available within the City, but on the countryside that was, on a clear day, visible from the heart of the potbanks and was within a few minutes drive in each direction. The Potters have always taken day trips into the countryside and most family photograph albums from the 1920s and 1930s onwards have their share of family snapshots taken in Dovedale, the

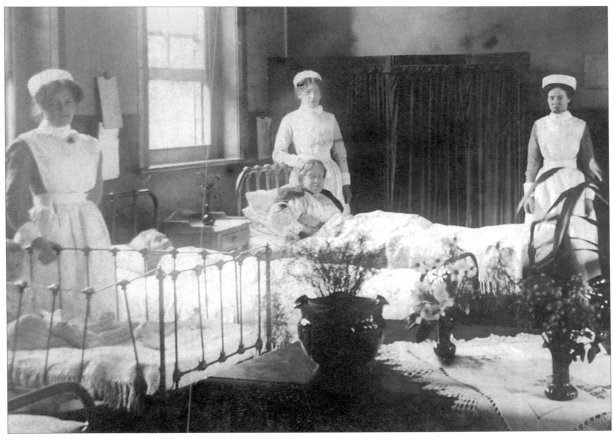

90 An early 20th-century photograph of a ward at the Westcliffe Hospital.

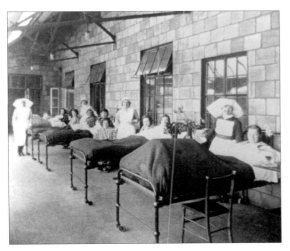

91 Two images of the tuberculosis ward at the City General Hospital in the 1930s. Fresh air was still considered a vital part of the treatment and wards had open verandahs on which patients slept. Note also the change in nursing uniforms.

Manifold Valley, up on the Staffordshire Moorlands, at the Roaches and at Rudyard Lake. They will also include photographs from Trentham. The Park continued to be the dominant attraction for the post-war generation of Potters. The Sutherlands had kept a sharehold in their former estate and, typically, had urged 'respectable' and 'improving' forms of recreation. By the 1960s, however, the Park was offering an experience that could compete with the growing seaside attractions at north

92 A photograph from the 1940s or 1950s with a typically grey scene over the canal. Notice the gas lamp standard.

93 The Coliseum in Hanley in 1938.

94 The Palace Entertainment Centre stands on the site of the city's first cinema, Barber's Picture Palace.

95 Unity House, the tallest single structure in the city. After accommodating City and County Council offices it is now empty and awaiting a decision over its future.

96   The swimming pool at Trentham, demolished in the 1980s.

Wales and Southport that were becoming so popular with pottery workers: boating, bowls, a miniature railway, golf, tennis, a swimming pool and a children's playground, in addition to the lake, the woods and the formal gardens. Jones noted that the Park attracted people of all ages, that there was something for everybody, but most importantly, and particularly on Trentham Thursday, it was a place you could meet members of the opposite sex. This broad appeal was capitalised on by the management of the Park, who promoted it as a family day out, a feature that may have contributed to its later demise as younger people sought refuge in places away from the family. By the early 1960s it was obvious the attraction needed to be brought up to date and the Sutherlands tried again to sell the park, failing

to do so until the 1980s. The ballroom was modernised and marketed as the place to be. The venue became popular for a number of bands including the Beatles and the Rolling Stones during their 1960s heyday.

Other forms of recreation were becoming available to the young people of Stoke-on-Trent. Not least of these was sport. The city has two major football clubs, Stoke City and Port Vale. The former had a long and fruitful connection with the great Sir Stanley Matthews, and rivalry between the teams has always been intense. The original Port Vale ground lies under what is now a part of the Potteries Shopping Centre, and the City has also, more recently, re-located from its Victoria Ground. The Victoria Ground was the oldest league ground in the world, matches having been

97 A view of Trentham Gardens showing some of the remaining buildings and the tranquillity which the place offered visitors.

98 The wide expanse that was the Victoria Ground, home of Stoke City. The stadium once dominated the surrounding community of terraced housing.

99 The Britannia Stadium, the new home of Stoke City. It reflects the fundamental changes in football during the last twenty years. A community of supporters living on the doorstep has been sacrificed. In its place will be a community of commerce using the stadium as a focus for investment and enterprise. As yet the ground remains remote from any community.

played there since the formation of the league in 1888. The first professional match at the ground was against West Bromwich Albion and it was against West Brom that Stoke City played their last league game at the Victoria Ground in 1997. During that time the sport had changed from that of the working class to big business. Football grounds were built within strong industrial communities and generated intense loyalties that often moulded the identity of the community. The stadium has now been demolished and the ground is derelict and

100 Parking is already becoming a problem in Market Place, Burslem, *c.*1950. The *Leopard Inn* can be seen in the middle of the picture.

101 Big Alf's Last Firing. The last firing of the kiln at the Gladstone Works in Longton was considered worthy enough for the national press to cover the story. It was the end of an era. *Courtesy of Denis Thorpe and The* Guardian.

overgrown beside the A500, the road that connects Stoke's two motorway junctions, leaving a gaping hole. The new Britannia Stadium, born from corporate ideals and still seen by many loyal Stoke fans as soul-less, sits gleaming across the other side of the dual carriageway, isolated from any community.

Speedway was another draw for post-war youth. The stadium at Sun Street became a regular venue on the circuit after 1958. The speed and the hint of danger had its allure and the participants were accessible to their fans. The younger people stood close to the track and, where possible, to the racers and identified with the competition and rivalries. The older spectators tended to be more interested in the machines. Whilst football fans simply donned their team's colours, speedway fans tried to merge the developing teenage emblems with those of the Potters. But the intensity failed to match that of the football crowd and speedway has suffered from fluctuating support and sponsorship.

102 Public art has not always met with approval. The statue of Sir Stanley Matthews is widely accepted but the ceramic benches in Hanley have not enjoyed the same level of success. The bench in Stoke churchyard seems to go unnoticed for the most part.

103 The School of Art and Library, Stoke.

104   Vale Place in Hanley in 1961. The waste tip from Hanley Deep Pit dominates the scene.

During the 1960s music emerged as a major force and Trentham became the obvious focus for large concerts after the appearances by the likes of the Beatles, so that before becoming 'stadium' acts and huge corporate enterprises bands such as Oasis and Radiohead played there. Smaller venues in the city have endured mixed fortunes, often the place to play on a tour building up to major stardom, but afterwards too small to accommodate the bands. The *Wheatsheaf* in Stoke was host to many major acts (Oasis played there to an audience of less than fifty) before it lost a promotions battle to *The Stage* in Hanley.

Nightclubs have been a significant feature in the social life of Stoke. During the 1940s and

105 St Paul's Church, Burslem in 1959, as seen from Newcastle Street.

1950s dancehalls could be found in all of the six towns. Young people in particular met with groups of friends to go dancing. In Hanley they gathered above the Regent/Gaumont cinema. The dances on a Saturday night started at about

> 8.00pm and usually featured a local big band. There was usually an interval during which time people flocked to the Bird in Hand pub that once stood opposite the Theatre Royal. They sat on the back stairs, many of them too young to be drinking alcohol. The dancehall sold only soft drinks.

In the mid-1960s a new force emerged in the local dance scene at the *Golden Torch* in Hose Street, Tunstall. The opening night featured Billy J. Kramer and the Dakotas. By the end of the decade the club was known for its soul music. During the 1970s it featured live performances by the likes of Ben E. King and the Drifters, but was by then renowned for its northern soul and all-night sessions. It closed as a nightclub in the mid-1970s and the building was burnt down several years later. The club became a nationally recognised venue, people travelling from all over the country to experience the northern soul, but it was also a focus for local young people, integral to the identity of Tunstall and, by default, the city as a whole. If you considered yourself apart of the youth movement, you had to go to the Torch. It was a society within society, with its own rules and conventions.

106 (above) Number 63 York Street, Hanley, 1959. As the road sweeper tended to the by-ways, a lady kept her windows meticulously clean.

107 (left) A typical potter's cart abandoned and decaying in 1960. Such carts were once common on the streets, carrying waste or small quantities of raw materials or ware.

The impact of the City's Cultural Quarter has yet to be felt within the city, let alone regionally or nationally. The concept has had a difficult brief from its inception. Manchester and Birmingham are within easy reach and are much more substantial cultural magnets than Stoke-on-Trent. Despite this, the Quarter is the most significant regeneration project in the city.

The Sentinel, the local newspaper, reported in 2000 that the pottery industry's workforce

108 A more recent and very personal view of the potbanks by Donald Morris. For this well-known local photographer, the image symbolises the decline of the industry and the loss of much of the City's heritage.

was reduced from 30,000 in the 1980s to 17,000 in 1999. Unlike other conurbations, Stoke has not attracted significant jobs in other industries to compensate for this decline, to which must be added the recent losses of the coal and steel industries. The six towns have maintained their historical rivalry, which has led to many debates about where regeneration grants should be applied. The development of Hanley as the commercial centre has resulted in the decline of the shopping centres in the other five towns, although this occurred much longer ago than is generally assumed. Even by the middle of the 19th century,

109 The workplaces within the potbanks changed very little until comparatively recently. This is Price & Kensington, Middleport.

Hanley was a superior shopping centre to Burslem or even the neighbouring borough of Newcastle-under-Lyme. The council was right to approve plans to increase and develop the amount of space available to what may be termed the 'consumption' industries, shopping facilities, restaurants, cultural centres and theatres, but the choice of Hanley only added

to the resentment felt in the other towns. Consumption industries have been vital to the successful regeneration of other cities as the cases of Sheffield and Nottingham clearly illustrate, each of which has something unique to offer tourists and outside investors. These qualities may be historical or they may have been conceived in modern times. Critics of

110 A back alley in Fenton. Obvious modernisations at the potbank contrast with the traditional bottle ovens.

111 Allotments have always been popular in industrialised areas. Stoke-on-Trent is no exception. Today the allotments are as much a recreation and means of socialising as they were once an important way of supplementing meagre diets. The Sideway allotments have been removed since this photograph was taken.

112 A view across open waste ground towards the Michelin works at Stoke.

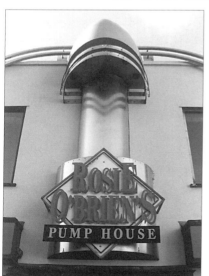

113 The Chicago Rock Café and Rosie O'Brien's Pump House represent recent trends away from large nightclubs towards a scene focused on a bar.

114 The Place, for many years the cornerstone of nightlife in Hanley, continues to attract huge crowds despite increasing opposition.

the Stoke Cultural Quarter claim the original vision was too focused on the local. The report *Major Touring Venues for Stoke-on-Trent*, published in 1993, concluded that, for an area with a possible catchment of about one million people, there was serious under-investment in the performing arts. The council decided to pivot the cultural quarter on the redevelopment of the Regent Theatre and the Victoria Hall and to attract higher quality restaurants with the redesign of Piccadilly.

Piccadilly was once a thriving centre at the core of the local 'monkey run', the almost ritual walk from the town centre to Hope Street during which young men and women hoped to find a mate. Today it is dominated by the Regent Theatre, an enterprise run by a partnership between the City Council and the Ambassador Group. The theatre, or cinema as it was at the time of its closure, was redesigned to accommodate touring shows, particularly from the West End. Its emergence undoubtedly impacted on the Theatre Royal, that has since re-opened as a nightclub. Surrounding the Regent are numerous snack bars and restaurants, many providing street side tables. There are also exclusive designer clothes outlets along the now pedestrianised road.

115 The refurbished Regent Theatre dominates the skyline of the City's Cultural Quarter. The Theatre was designed to take full productions direct from the West End.

It could be argued that the city has not yet matched its investment in cultural facilities with any move to redefine the job market in Stoke towards the post-industrial. Local people still feel isolated from the lifestyles and jobs associated with heritage and culture. It has been a mark of the success of Stoke's neighbours that their citizens have adapted to the new post-industrial economy. This is the challenge facing the modern city.

Notes

1 EARLY HISTORY, PP.1–7
1. G. Clark, *Prehistoric England*, 1962, p.49.
2. Cited in W. Klemperer and A. Parkes, *Berryhill Fields – history and archaeology*, Millennium Project for Stoke-on-Trent, 2000.
3. M.W. Greenslade, *A History of Stoke-upon-Trent*, Staffordshire County Library, 1985, an extract from *The Victoria History of the County of Staffordshire Volume VIII*, ed. J.G. Jenkins, University of London Institute of Historical Research, 1963.
4. R. Talbot, *The Church and Ancient Parish of Stoke-upon-Trent*, Stoke-on-Trent, 1969.
5. M.J. Branney, *The Ornamental Building Stones of Stoke-on-Trent*, Staffordshire Geological Recording Scheme Publication No.1, City Museum and Art Gallery, Hanley, Stoke-on-Trent, 1983.
6. J. Ward, *The Borough of Stoke-upon-Trent*, republished by Webberley Ltd, Stoke-on-Trent, 1984, p.464.

2 THE MEDIEVAL PERIOD, PP.8–19
1. D.M. Palliser, *The Staffordshire Landscape*, Hodder and Stoughton, London, 1976, p.60.
2. M.W. Greenslade, *A History of Hanley*, Staffordshire County Library, 1983, an extract from *The Victoria History of the County of Staffordshire Volume VIII*, p.151.
3. J.H.Y. Briggs, *A History of Longton*, Department of Adult Education, University of Keele, 1982.
4. N. Pevsner, *The Buildings of England – Staffordshire*, Penguin, Harmondsworth, 1974, p.208.
5. J.L. Tomkinson, *A History of Hulton Abbey*, Staffordshire Archaeological Studies No. 10, City Museum and Art Gallery, Stoke-on-Trent, 1997, p.15.
6. Tomkinson, *Hulton Abbey*, p.22.
7. F. Hughes, *Mother Town – episodes in the history of Burslem*, Burslem Community Development Trust, 2000, p.11.
8. A. Taylor, *Stoke-on-Trent: a Pictorial History*, Phillimore, Chichester, 1995, pp.2–3.
9. Tomkinson, *Hulton Abbey*, p.23.
10. W. Klemperer and N. Boothroyd, *Excavations at Hulton Abbey, Staffordshire*

1987-94, Society for Medieval Archaeology, in preparation.

11. J. Steed, *Trentham – a church through history*, Panda Press, Stone, 1994, p.24.

12. Palliser, *Staffordshire Landscape*, p.77.

13. W. Klemperer and A. Parkes, *Berryhill Fields*, p.6.

14. Klemperer and Parkes, *Berryhill Fields*, p.17.

15. J.G. Jenkins, *A History of Newcastle-under-Lyme*, Staffordshire County Library, 1983, an extract from *The Victoria History of the County of Staffordshire Volume VIII*, ed. J.G. Jenkins, University of London Institute of Historical Research, 1963, p.5.

16. Palliser, *Staffordshire Landscape*, p.80.

17. Palliser, *Staffordshire Landscape*, p.82.

18. Talbot, *Church and Ancient Parish*, p.8.

19. *Coal Mines in Staffordshire*, Local History Source Book No.3, Staffordshire County Council Education Department, 1968, p.3.

20. Palliser, *Staffordshire Landscape*, p.109.

3   SECULAR GROWTH AND CIVIL STRIFE, PP.20-4

1. Steed, *Trentham*, p.31.

2. Tomkinson, *Hulton Abbey*, p.43.

3. Tomkinson, *Hulton Abbey*, p.66.

4. Pevsner, *Staffordshire*, p.25.

5. Taylor, *A Pictorial History*, p.3.

6. Tomkinson, *Hulton Abbey*, p.67.

7. Hughes, *Mother Town*, p.19.

8. J. Smith and T. Randall (eds.), *Kill or Cure: medical remedies of the 16th and 17th centuries from the Staffordshire Record Office*, Staffordshire Record Office, 1987, p.42, D1287/20/2 (1683).

9. R. Talbot, *Penkhull Remembered Again*, Cartwright Bros., Stoke-on-Trent, 1980, p.24.

10. Klemperer and Parkes, *Berryhill Fields*, p.18.

11. Klemperer and Parkes, *Berryhill Fields*, p.23.

12. M.W. Greenslade, *A History of Tunstall*, Staffordshire County Library, 1981, an extract from *The Victoria History of the County of Staffordshire Volume VIII*, ed. J.G. Jenkins, University of London Institute of Historical Research, 1963, p.99.

4   URBANISATION AND INDUSTRIAL REVOLUTION, PP.25–49

1. Pevsner, *Staffordshire*, p.309.

2. Taylor, *A Pictorial History*, p.1.

3. J. Aitkin, *The Country Around Manchester 1795*, p.518, cited in Greenslade, *History of Tunstall*, p.81.

4. Ward, *Borough of Stoke*, p.88.

5. B. Young and J.G. Jenkins, *A History of Fenton*, 1984, an extract from *The*

Victoria History of the County of Staffordshire Volume VIII, ed. J.G. Jenkins, University of London Institute of Historical Research, 1963, p.208.

6. Palliser, *Staffordshire Landscape*, p.236.
7. W.J. Thompson, *Industrial Archaeology of North Staffordshire*, Moorland Publishing Company, p.23.
8. C. Hawke-Smith, *The Making of the Six Towns*, City Museum and Art Gallery, Stoke-on-Trent, 1985, p.30.
9. A.J. Taylor, *The Staffordshire Coal Industry*, Staffordshire County Library 1981, an extract from *The Victoria History of the County of Staffordshire Volume II*, ed. M.W Greenslade and J.G. Jenkins, University of London Institute of Historical Research, 1967, p.74.
10. Young and Jenkins, *History of Fenton*, p.244.
11. Young and Jenkins, *History of Fenton*, p.245.
12. *State of Large Towns in Staffordshire*, Staffordshire County Council Education Department, Local History Source Book G.12, 1972, p.1.
13. Sentinel Centenary 1854–1954, *Rendezvous with the Past*, Staffordshire Sentinel Newspapers Ltd, Hanley, 1954, p.43.
14. Hawke-Smith, *Making of the Six Towns*, p.34.
15. E.J.D. Warrilow, *History of Etruria*, Staffordshire, England, 1760–1951, Etruscan Publications, Stoke-on-Trent, 1952, p.23.
16. *State of Large Towns in Staffordshire*, p.13.
17. *Poor Relief in Staffordshire 1662–1840*, Staffordshire County Council Education Department, Local History Source Book G.2, 1975, p.22.
18. Thompson, *Industrial Archaeology*, p.122.
19. *Poor Relief in Staffordshire*, p.7.
20. S. Shaw, *History of the Staffordshire Potters*, cited in R. Talbot, *Penkhull Remembered*, p.61.
21. D. Baker, *Workhouses in the Potteries*, City of Stoke-on-Trent Historic Buildings Survey, 1984, p.35.
22. Palliser, *Staffordshire Landscape*, p.138.
23. Greenslade, *A History of Hanley*, p.154.
24. Taylor, *A Pictorial History*, p.33.
25. Greenslade, *A History of Stoke-upon-Trent*, p.190.
26. Ward, *Borough of Stoke*, p.212.
27. Pevsner, *Staffordshire*, p.254.
28. Ward, *Borough of Stoke*, p.241.
29. E.J.D. Warrilow, *Arnold Bennett and Stoke-on-Trent*, Etruscan Publications, Hanley, 1966, p.18.

5 WEALTH AND WELFARE, PP.50–67

1. Pevsner, *Staffordshire*, pp.283-5.
2. M. Drabble, *Arnold Bennett*, Weidenfeld and Nicolson, London, 1974, p.159.

3. A. Bennett, *The Card*, Methuen, 1911, cited in T. Carter, *The Crusade Against Crippledom*, North Staffordshire Medical Institute, Stoke-on-Trent, 1991, p.12

4. Carter, *Crusade Against Crippledom*, p.24.

5. A. Taylor, *A Century of The Potteries*, Sutton Publishing, Stroud, 2000, p.27.

6. Cited in I. Lawley and A. Dobraszczyc, *Parks for the People*, City of Stoke-on-Trent, 1988, p.2.

7. Lawley and Dobraszczyc, *Parks for the People*, p.2.

8. P. Lead, *The Trent & Mersey Canal*, The Moorland Publishing Company, Ashbourne, 1980, p.14.

9. B. Jeuda, *Rudyard Lake 1797-1997*, Churnet Valley Books, Leek, 1997, p.25.

10. I. Lawley, *Potters' Holiday*, City Museum and Art Gallery, Stoke-on-Trent, p.6.

11. C.T. Goode, *Trentham – the Hall, Gardens and Branch Railway*, Hull, 1985, p.11.

6 THE MODERN ERA, PP.68-85

1. E. Fanshawe, *Penkhull Memories*, Staffordshire County Library, 1983, p.4.

2. A. Taylor, *Voices of the Potteries*, Tempus Publishing, Stroud, 2001, p.12.

3. Taylor, *Voices*, p.16.

4. Cited in Sentinel Centenary 1854–1954, *Rendezvous with the Past*, p.43.

5. P. Burns, *Memories of Stoke-on-Trent*, True North Books, Halifax, 1998.

6. Burns, *Memories*, p.15.

7. Sentinel Centenary 1854–1954, *Rendezvous with the Past*, p.65.

8. Taylor, *Century of the Potteries*, p.93.

9. E. Billington, *The Staffordshire Coalfields – North Staffordshire*, in J. Benson, *The Miners of Staffordshire, 1840-1914*, Centre for Local History, Keele University, Staffordshire Heritage Series No.4, p.10.

10. Billington, *Staffordshire Coalfields*, p.12.

11. Taylor, *Voices*, pp.17-18.

7 THE POST-MODERN ERA, PP.86-111

1. Taylor, *Voices*, p.68.

2. Taylor, *Voices*, p.68.

3. J.R. Powner, *A Duty Done – the history of Fire-fighting in Staffordshire*, Staffordshire County Council, 1987, p.128.

4. Taylor, *Century of the Potteries*, p.58.

5. Taylor, *Century of the Potteries*, p.59.

6. M. Jones, *Potbank*, Secker & Warburg, London, 1961.

7. Jones, *Potbank*.

Bibliography

Aitken, J., *The Country Around Manchester*, 1795

Baker, D., *Workhouses in the Potteries*, City of Stoke-on-Trent Historic Buildings Survey, 1984

Bennett, A., *The Card*, Methuen, 1911

Billington, E., *The Staffordshire Coalfields – North Staffordshire*, in J. Benson, *The Miners of Staffordshire 1840-1914*, Staffordshire Heritage Series No. 4, Centre for Local History, Keele University

Boothroyd, N., *Hulton Abbey Small Finds*, www.stoke.gov.uk/museums/pmag/archaeology/fieldarchaeology/rephult.htm

Branney, M.J., *The Ornamental Building Stones of Stoke-on-Trent*, Staffordshire Geological Recording Scheme Publication No. 1, City Museum and Art Gallery, Hanley, Stoke-on-Trent, 1983

Briggs, J.H.Y., *A History of Longton*, Department of Adult Education, University of Keele, 1982

Burns, P., *Memories of Stoke-on-Trent*, True North Books, Halifax, 1998

Carter, T., *The Crusade Against Crippledom*, North Staffordshire Medical Institute, Stoke-on-Trent, 1991

Drabble, M., *Arnold Bennett*, Weidenfeld and Nicolson, London, 1974

Fanshawe, E., *Penkhull Memories*, Staffordshire County Library, 1983

Goode, C.T., *Trentham – the Hall, Gardens and Branch Railway*, Hull, 1985

Greenslade, M.W., *A History of Hanley*, Staffordshire County Library, 1983, extracted from *The Victoria County History of Staffordshire Vol. VIII*, ed. J.G. Jenkins, Institute of Historical Research, University of London, 1963

Greenslade, M.W., *A History of Tunstall*, Staffordshire County Library, 1981, extracted from *The Victoria County History of Staffordshire Vol. VIII*, ed. J.G. Jenkins, Institute of Historical Research, University of London, 1963

Greenslade, M.W., *A History of Stoke-upon-Trent*, Staffordshire County Library, 1985, extracted from *The Victoria County History of Staffordshire Vol. VIII*, ed. J.G. Jenkins, Institute of Historical Research, University of London, 1963

Hawke-Smith, C., *The Making of the Six Towns*, City Museum and Art Gallery, Hanley, Stoke-on-Trent, 1985

Hughes, F., *Mother Town – episodes in the history of Burslem*, Burslem Community Development Trust, 2000

Jenkins, J.G., *A History of Newcastle-under-Lyme*, Staffordshire County Library, 1983, extracted from *The Victoria County History of Staffordshire Vol. VIII*, ed. J.G. Jenkins, Institute of Historical Research, University of London, 1963

Jeuda, B., *Rudyard Lake 1797-1997*, Churnet Valley Books, Leek, 1997

Jones, M., *Potbank*, Secker & Warburg, London, 1961

Karena, J., Latimer, C. and Beard, M., *Images of the Potteries*, Breedon Books, Derby, 1999

Klemperer, W. and Parkes, A., *Berryhill Fields – history and archaeology*, Millennium Project, Stoke-on-Trent, 2000

Lawley, I., *Potters' Holiday*, City Museum and Art Gallery, Hanley, Stoke-on-Trent

Lawley, I. and Dobraszczyc, A., *Parks for the People*, Stoke-on-Trent, 1988

Lead, P., *The Trent & Mersey Canal*, Moorland Publishing Co., Ashbourne, 1988

Owen, D.E., *Staffordshire Waterways*, National Waterways Museum, Ellesmere Port, 1986

Palliser, D.M., *The Staffordshire Landscape*, Hodder and Stoughton, London, 1976

Pevsner, N., *The Buildings of England – Staffordshire*, Penguin, Harmondsworth, 1974

Plot, R., *The Natural History of Staffordshire*, 1686

Powner, J.R., *A Duty Done – the history of Fire-fighting in Staffordshire*, Staffordshire County Council, 1987

Shaw, S., *History of the Staffordshire Potters*, David and Charles Reprints, 1970 (original edition, 1829)

Smith, J. and Randall, T., *Kill or Cure: medical remedies of the 16th and 17th centuries from the Staffordshire Record Office*, Staffordshire Record Office, 1987

Speake, R.(ed.), *Audley*, Department of Adult Education, University of Keele, 1972

Staffordshire County Council Education Department, *Coal Mines in Staffordshire*, Local History Source Book No. 3, 1968

Staffordshire County Council Education Department, *State of Large Towns in Staffordshire*, Local History Source Book G. 12, 1972

Staffordshire County Council Education Department, *Poor Relief in Staffordshire 1662-1840*, Local History Source Book G. 2, 1975

Staffordshire Sentinel Newspapers, *Sentinel Centenary 1854-1954, rendezvous with the past*, Staffordshire Sentinel Newspapers, Stoke-on-Trent, 1954

Steed. J., *Trentham – a church through history*, Panda Press, Stone, 1994

Talbot, R., *The Church and Ancient Parish of Stoke-upon-Trent*, Stoke-on-Trent, 1969

Talbot, R., *Penkhull Remembered Again*, Cartwright Bros., Stoke-on-Trent, 1980

Taylor, A., *Stoke-on-Trent: a pictorial history*, Phillimore, Chichester, 1995

Taylor, A., *A Century of the Potteries*, Sutton Publishing, Stroud, 2000

Taylor, A., *Voices of the Potteries*, Tempus Publishing, Stroud, 2001

Taylor, A.J., *The Staffordshire Coal Industry*, Staffordshire County Library, 1981, extracted from *The Victoria County History of Staffordshire Vol. II*, ed. M.W. Greenslade and J.G. Jenkins, Institute of Historical Research, University of London, 1963

Thompson, W.J., *Industrial Archaeology of North Staffordshire*, Moorland Publishing Co., 1974

Tomkinson, J.L., *A History of Hulton Abbey*, Staffordshire Archaeological Studies No. 10, City Museum and Art Gallery, Hanley, Stoke-on-Trent, 1997

Ward, J., *The Borough of Stoke-upon-Trent*, republished by Webberley Ltd, Stoke-on-Trent, 1984

Warrilow, E.J.D., *History of Etruria, Staffordshire, England 1760-1951*, Etruscan Publications, Stoke-on-Trent, 1952

Warrilow, E.J.D., *Arnold Bennett and Stoke-on-Trent*, Etruscan Publications, Stoke-on-Trent, 1966

Young, B. and Jenkins, J.G., *A History of Fenton*, Staffordshire County Library, 1984, extracted from *The Victoria County History of Staffordshire Vol. VIII*, ed. J.G. Jenkins, Institute of Historical Research, University of London, 1963

Index

Page references to illustrations are given in **bold**.